More Than Words

The Freedom to Thrive After Trauma

Margaret M. Vasquez

Licensed Professional Clinical Counselor

Certified Trauma Therapist

Certified Intensive Trauma Therapy Instructor

Foreword by Thomas Lee Reynolds, M.D.

Culture of Connection
P.O. Box 724
Steubenville, OH 43952

Printed in the United States.

ISBN-13: 978-1720525486
ISBN-10: 172052548X

I've referred many people to this program with varying issues: birth trauma, abuse histories of all sorts, physical issues, with varying degrees of abilities and 'stuckness.' Each one was freed through treatment to reach their potential. I am not aware of a more effective, efficient treatment for trauma. Transformed lives are the norm!
    - BR, Attorney

In all my many years in physical medicine, I have never seen such dynamic change in patients in such a short period of time as a result of incorporating this technique with viscerosomatic treatment. It's time for any and every form of patient care to incorporate this methodology as an integral part of holistic care, especially for those patients with prior unmanageable conditions.
    - Robert C. Marrow, D.C.

I was at my wit's end dealing with our 14-year-old adopted daughter. We had been doing attachment therapy since she was seven years old. Things had gotten so bad that we contacted a therapeutic boarding school. As a last-ditch effort, we decided to try Thrive Trauma Recovery with Margaret Vasquez. It worked! The change was immediate, and I can honestly say that I am enjoying the relationship I now have with my daughter. I am still in awe!
    - Adoptive Mother, Ohio

As a professional working in the field of foster care and adoption, I recommend Margaret Vasquez's trauma therapy services to clients on a regular basis. As a mother of children suffering from complex trauma, I was blessed to connect with Thrive Trauma Recovery on a personal level. Processing through the trauma your child has experienced is a necessary first step for them to start healing. Thrive Trauma Recovery therapists give traumatized children a safe place to share their stories of when they were brave, receive praise for being strong, and process with parents how they can be a support to their children. While my husband and I know we have a long road ahead of us, we are forever grateful for the treatment our daughter received and are ready to walk with her on her journey of healing.

- **Danielle Miller, MSW, LSW**
  Caring for Kids, Inc.
  Clinical Case Managers

I think now, looking back, we did not fight the enemy; we fought ourselves. And the enemy was in us...those of us who did make it have an obligation to build again, to teach to others what we know, and to try with what's left of our lives to find a goodness and a meaning to this life.
- Chris Taylor, *Platoon*

Dedication

To Bev,

whose friendship has taught me

the meaning of connection.

Foreword

I first met Margaret when searching for an out-of-the box therapist who could help my adopted autistic son. He sees the world in a "different way". He is a bundle of words, creativity and opinions. Sadly, he was also massively abused before adoption in most every way imaginable. My son is quite verbal and articulate, though often he can't get the concepts beneath these words due to his type of autism. Once a special education teacher had told my wife and I that my son was stuck up. When I enquired why, she said, "Because he uses words which the other students in the class don't understand". I told her, "Ma'am my wife has two master's degrees and I am a physician/child psychiatrist who was on staff at Harvard Medical School. That is how we talk at home." We were used to people misunderstanding him; somedays we struggled ourselves with comprehending him. After asking my colleagues for a therapist who used techniques other than the traditional talking therapies, we found Margaret.

My son immediately took to Margaret. She has a spritely wisdom about her, at the same time she is still and dancing with ideas. My son liked that he would be able to create with Margaret, who encouraged this expression. She worked with him in her unique way, and we saw him settle down. He talked to us of stories, drawings and even a videotape. We saw that he lowered his state of continual fear. (At times, we called him privately the "Master of Disaster" because he was so hypervigilant that he could take a balmy day and imagine connections that ended in

Armageddon!) My son became more comfortable "in his skin". He listened to us when we told him he was safe, and he was able to talk about his past without devolving into panic. I knew then Margaret had hold of a magical process that could change the way we see treatment of traumatized persons.

I have a lot of experience with traditional mental health. I was the protégé of Sigmund Freud's protégé's, protégé: fourth generation Freud. I had been the Medical Director of the largest treatment center for abused children in the city of Boston and had directed the State Hospital program for the Commonwealth of Massachusetts amongst other leadership positions. We had moved from Boston to Ohio for the good of the family, and I had feared that I was leaving innovation. I was definitely wrong.

Margaret presents as the voice of a new technique for reaching traumatized persons, which combines the logical properties of the left-brain hemisphere with the raw experience of the right brain where a decade earlier we had realized that traumatic memories reside. Unfortunately, the majority of therapists were still using left-sided brain techniques, and missing the need to reach the other hemisphere. Margaret had spent over a decade learning from her mentors and refining techniques to develop "Neuro Reformatting and Integration" (NRI). At the same time she was a prophet for many desperate families, she was also a heretic within established mental health professional circles. *After all, how could significant trauma be processed in just a week? Wasn't understanding all of the details of the trauma and connecting them to the whole of the person's subsequent life necessary for self-actualization? Moreover, how could people go through NRI without writhing from the pain of re-experiencing the very horrors of their past that their mind had developed defenses to avoid? It just wasn't possible...*but I had seen it work. Surely such a different way of approaching psychosocial trauma couldn't be scientific.

Let's turn to science to understand how her theories fit in psychological research. Many people fear science. They see it as either systematically eroding religious beliefs or as a future without a conscience. These fears are far from the truth. At its essence, science sets up a simple way to observe the world and understand its connections. By setting up an "experiment" where certain parts are watched systematically, scientists say that we understand how the physical world really works. Most people don't realize that progress in science is usually not from an Einstein who makes an intellectual leap from traditional wisdom. Rather, science is built on micro-innovations, shared with other scientists through publications and meetings. Another scientific team somewhere else in the world then builds upon this one small advancement. It is a slow, often frustrating, push toward deeper understanding.

When a seemingly new approach, like NRI, comes on the scene other professionals/social scientists, can be skeptical of its validity. However, NRI is built on several decades of work that integrates other scientific discoveries to find a better way to help the billions of traumatized people in the world. Most of these people have been so hurt by life that their potential is trapped. They often live in constant agony of the abuse, as if it was replaying like a perpetual "Groundhog Day" movie of cruelty.

Trauma occurs when the objective reality of a situation is so horribly overwhelming that it disrupts our cognitive, emotional and social functioning. Essentially the horror of "subjective" trauma events overwhelms the ability of our brain to objectively process the world and in that way, our perception becomes distorted and driven by events long since past. Moreover, our ability to use social relationships to heal (which is a basic means of reestablishing harmony in our brains) becomes highly suspect. *If I was hurt by people whom I should have been able to trust, how can I trust anyone else?* So goes the logic of trauma. People then become disconnected from their emotions, others and ultimately themselves.

Connectedness is increasingly being studied. I was listening to National Public Radio the other day and it described how trees are connected ecologically. Fascinatingly, in one experiment radioactive chemicals were given to one tree and these particles showed up in surrounding trees quite far away. Scientists realized that a tree shares its biochemical reality with other trees. Curiously, this sharing was not species-specific; a maple tree freely communicates with an oak, birch and beech tree in the general vicinity.

When scientists tried to unravel the mechanism for this communication, they found that the roots of trees are interconnected. Fascinatingly the connection is actually made by small tubes in fungus, which transfer chemicals from one root system to another tree's root system. The tree provides photosynthetically engineered sugars for the fungi, and the fungi connect trees and mine little deposits of minerals to feed the trees. This set of tree connections has been termed the "Wood Wide Web". *Who says scientists don't have a sense of humor!*

Our brains, like the trees, are interconnected. Our brain is an ecology of connections. We are much more than a sum of our parts. Neuroscientists for the past two decades have known that we are born with more brain "wires" than we will ever use. A person's experience reinforces certain brain connections and wires. The reinforced connections grow stronger while the little-used connections start physically to wither away. In this way our brains become an ecosystem, and we become "ourselves".

Trauma fundamentally hijacks this brain development. Instead of a natural network of brain connections, trauma interrupts the normal brain processing of signals. These interruptions in turn become reinforced and further misshape the brain from its original potential "form". In such a way, the neurological landscape of the brain in a traumatized individual becomes malformed by the trauma.

Brain science is starting to perceive these pathways. We are realizing that cells from one region actually connect to anatomically separate regions of the brain. We know this through the development of images called "Connectomes". NRI is undoubtedly working on these connections, either chemically at or inside the cell, or more broadly through the ways that groups of cells "talk" to other groups of cells.

Historians of science tell us that after building knowledge little by little, other scientists see a new way to put this information together. I believe NRI is such a shift.

- NRI is a new method of treating trauma which connects the right and left hemispheres of the brain with inputs from the midbrain where emotions and memory are stored

- NRI uses the different strengths of each hemisphere to develop a logical understanding of the trauma, and thereby allow the person to feel more connected to his or her own body and past, and to not be haunted by trauma.

- NRI has good "face value". It is a technique that is logical, fits recent neuroscience discoveries, and makes sense to the traumatized person.

- Finally, NRI does not rely on esoteric theories, which are intellectual abstractions of a person's direct life experience. Traumatized persons understand the process – its methods and goals.

I encourage you to think "out-of-the-box" and consider this innovative way of healing trauma. I have spent my professional life working with some of the most mentally damaged people – genetically, traumatically and behaviorally. I have found that the people who do better consistently make sense of their life and work to better their lot in life. Traumatized persons who join in NRI therapy leave the therapy more informed about themselves and motivated to build their lives forward. What more could we ask?

Thomas (Lee) Reynolds, MD
Child & Adolescent, Adult & Addiction Psychiatrist
June 1, 2018

Preface

For sixteen years of my life, I exhausted my resources of time, money and hope, trying desperately to find relief from the myriad and confounding effects of trauma. It was a long, dark, and arduous route that, though I do not regret it, I would never wish on anyone. Throughout that time, I strained to make sense of the torment I was experiencing. I read book after book, but found no answers. How had I become so lost in such deep woods? I longed for a map or even a trail of breadcrumbs.

When I finally received real and lasting help, I dedicated myself to helping others who, like me, were seeking freedom from the pain and confusion that trauma brings. Sadly, most people tend to shake their heads and assume victims will be permanently scarred by traumatic events. This book is a line in the sand to trauma. There is a boundary that trauma cannot cross. There is effective treatment and there is hope. Freedom awaits.

Acknowledgements

It is impossible for me to adequately convey the honor it has been to work with traumatized people over the course of my counseling practice. I've witnessed the struggle and the victory of those willing to reach in faith beyond surviving, with the conviction that they were created to live a thriving life. Walking that leg of the journey with others is edifying and has convinced me of the indomitable nature of the human spirit. The characters, situations and results from treatment described herein are factual, with the identifying information having been changed to protect the anonymity of these brave individuals.

I will always be grateful to the late Louis Tinnin, M.D. and Linda Gantt, Ph.D., ATR-BC, whose work freed me from the darkest point in my life and upon which my work is based. Without their role in my life, I would not have enjoyed the great privilege of bringing this work to the world. For all those who supported me in those bleak and desperate times, without you I would not have lived to help others or to write this book you hold. With a lump in my throat, I thank you. You will never be forgotten.

In the production of this book, I'm grateful to Ron Mazellan for the artwork on the cover. This picture initially came into my possession on a graduation card, and I was immediately struck by how perfectly it expresses the heavy load that trauma is. The picture has been in my office from the time I first began to practice counseling and is my way of inviting clients to unburden themselves of the traumas they carry, regardless of how isolated they have felt.

Thank you also to Ruth Aubrey, Paul Vasquez, Dennis Welch and many others for assistance with the editing; To Bev Richards, my gratitude for your cover design, serving as a sounding board and your tireless support. Lee Reynolds, M.D., I am grateful for your feedback. Your encouragement was timely at a point when I had grown weary of the production process.

Table of Contents

1	**My Story**	**1**
2	**The Backstory**	**7**
3	**Overcoming Aunt Betsy**	**17**
4	**Making Trauma History**	**25**
5	**How Trauma Works**	**30**
6	**Freedom from Trauma Messages**	**40**
7	**Emotions, Connection, & Power**	**50**
8	**Success Stories**	**64**
9	**Decoding Dynamics**	**87**
10	**What's Different About This Method?**	**120**
11	**Where Do I Go From Here?**	**127**

1

My Story

Fourteen years ago, on December 1, 2003, I very reluctantly drove my old, VW Jetta from Steubenville, OH down to Morgantown, WV to attend a two-week intensive outpatient trauma treatment program. When my therapist, Rachel, had mentioned it to me, I concluded (wrongly) that she had given up on me. I felt rejected and abandoned. I knew that I must be a very difficult client. I was meeting with her two or even three times a week just to stay alive. I was imminently suicidal and had been for 18 months, but I was a dedicated and motivated client. How could this be so difficult? Was I broken beyond repair? Were the mental health professionals all just too afraid to be honest and tell me? Were they too naively optimistic to face it themselves? I couldn't really blame Rachel. I was sure that I was probably burning her out.

All I knew was that I was in pain, a tremendous amount of emotional pain. I felt tormented. I agonized regularly trying to find a reason for it, but nothing in my life at the time was that bad other than the psychological pain itself. Every now and then, the pain would stop for a while. Sometimes the reprieve was a few days or sometimes even a few months, but the one certainty was that it would return with ferocity. By the time Rachel referred me to the Trauma Recovery Institute in Morgantown, West Virginia I had been in counseling for 16 years, hospitalized twice and misdiagnosed as having bipolar disorder. I had been prescribed various medications in all sorts of combinations. It felt like a long and torturous guessing game, and I felt like a lab rat with no obvious way out of the maze. None of the medications helped, and I was unable to metabolize many of them. The side effects were brutal, and I often felt like I had a heavy, wet wool blanket over my consciousness, as though the cogs of my mind were trying to turn through wet cement.

I was halfway through getting a Master of Arts in Counseling that I was sure I'd never be healthy enough to use. Besides, in good conscience I couldn't become a therapist because, in my heart of hearts, I didn't really believe it worked. The only reason I had entered the program at Franciscan University was because I didn't want to live on public assistance any longer. I had been homeless for a few weeks at some point in all the tumultuous years and at another point was receiving disability assistance from the government, but accepting those benefits went against everything in me. I wanted to be able to pay my own way. More than anything, I wanted to be able to contribute to society, but pursuing my counseling degree wasn't about becoming a therapist at all. I was simply trying to buy time while I figured out what in the world was wrong with me.

I had graduated from Franciscan years before with an undergraduate degree. It was certainly the scenic route through college. I showed up on campus only four months after running away from home and with a long list of traumas that only continued to grow with time. Paying attention in class, being able to apply myself and reach my potential academically, was unspeakably difficult, but I was like the frog in the pot of water. They say that if you put a frog in a pot of hot water, then the frog will jump out of the pot immediately. If you slowly turn up the heat, then he won't jump out of the pot. He'll just stay in there and cook to death. What I now call traumas had been commonplace in childhood and throughout my life up to that point. No bells went off in me that told me I needed trauma treatment. I didn't know there was such a thing. Even from what I was taught in the classroom as a counseling student, I was led to believe that trauma was all about military combat. I mean, isn't that what post-traumatic stress disorder is all about? Isn't that the diagnosis for those who fought in wars?

I had amassed a huge debt of student loans and was no closer to relief from my suffering. I pulled up to the treatment center in West Virginia that cold December morning and as I did, *Rescue Me* by Fontella Bass was playing on the radio. I remember thinking that I desperately needed someone to rescue *me* from having to go in that building for treatment for the next two weeks. As it turned out, getting this form of therapy was exactly what did rescue me. I had no hopes that this last ditch effort would help. Of all the factors surrounding attending intensive therapy (the cost of treatment, travel, hotel, and meals), the most expensive part was hope. On that front, I was completely bankrupt. I had been in therapy for a little over half of my life. I had seen innumerable psychologists, psychiatrists, counselors and social workers. I had been a determined client. I would pay for treatment out of my own pocket before I would buy food. I reasoned that I would rather be sane and hungry than crazy with a full belly. The 18 months leading up to that point, I was sitting in counseling classes and plotting how I would kill myself and when I would do it. Yet, professors and students alike would often tell me that I had such a peace about me. It made me at once feel relieved that they didn't know what I was thinking and terribly disconnected to be so unknown.

I had no idea what this treatment was all about. I had only been told that it was based on the directed use of art therapy. "Draw butterflies and flowers and I'm somehow going to feel differently about all of this crap?" I thought. They are crazier than I am. Even if this treatment did work for other people, I was sure it wouldn't work for me. None of the outpatient counseling, hospitalizations or medication had. Why would this be any different? I spent every day, and would often wake up at night, trying to understand what in the world was wrong. Oftentimes, my heart was wax, melting in my chest. My brain was taffy being pulled and gathered, pulled and gathered. It was a senseless endeavor, but my therapist insisted that I attend intensive treatment. I had no other choice. She didn't feel qualified to continue treating me. I decided to comply and give it my full effort. I reasoned God would know that I had tried everything and would be less offended when I killed myself. I didn't want to hurt others, but I couldn't continue any longer. My soul had third degree burns. I had been running on fumes for years. This was the end of the line. I expected to give this treatment my all, have it not work, and commit suicide.

As a counseling student, I knew that bipolar disorder was not what I was experiencing. I tried discussing that with all the many therapists and doctors I had met since the time of my misdiagnosis seven years prior. Their eyes would glaze over, as they would write out the prescription for the psychotropic medication of the week. After all, I was a mental patient. Why should they believe me? Rachel would tell me that it wasn't a likable diagnosis. She didn't understand that I didn't like it because it didn't fit. I felt like I was in an unbreakable, soundproof glass bubble and no matter how hard I shouted and pounded I couldn't be heard. I knew my own internal experience, and it didn't match the copious information I read about the diagnosis. Finally, one day Rachel was having lunch with a child psychiatrist friend of hers and was discussing my case, no doubt because I was exhausting her. Her friend told her that I didn't sound like I was bipolar. The psychiatrist told her I sounded like I had "enough PTSD to sink a battleship." At last someone got it. Even if this treatment was ridiculous and a waste of time, money, effort and hope, at least one of the professionals understood.

I attended a two-week intensive outpatient regimen of trauma therapy with Louis Tinnin, M.D and Linda Gantt, Ph.D., ATR-BC. From the beginning something was different. They explained to me why trauma causes such a lasting impact. They explained that it was biological and had to do with how the brain functions. My thinking felt very muddled and much of the explanation was lost on me. I didn't understand, but I understood that they understood and that was enough for me. We worked systematically through the traumas on the docket. By the end of the two weeks, I was raring to go. I wanted to become a trauma therapist as quickly as possible. It was almost impossible to articulate, but I had far greater mental clarity than I'd had in a very long time. I didn't have the feeling of constant emotional torment I had come to associate with being alive. I no longer wanted to die, not even a little bit. I learned that since trauma is biological, effective trauma therapy needed to be biological, too. Over the course of those two weeks my hair had turned to tiny little curls, and it stayed like that for the next year and a half. My doctor told me that when the storage of memories is reorganized it could shift hormones. That sudden hormonal shift caused the curling of my hair. The lesson of how interwoven we are physically, emotionally and spiritually was impressed upon me over and over, every time I caught a glimpse of my reflection.

2

The Backstory

Louis Tinnin, M.D. and Linda Gantt, Ph.D., ATR-BC developed the Instinctual Trauma Response (ITR) model of trauma treatment. It was, literally, their brainchild. Based on the instinctual response we have to any type of trauma Pierre Janet had written about over a hundred years ago, they developed that therapeutic approach while working at an inpatient unit for veterans and have produced outcome studies showing the effectiveness of the treatment.

While retaining all the essential aspects of the ITR model, I amended and added many components to the treatment in order to take into account my specialty, the client's experience. Over the years, I discussed the changes to the application of the method with my predecessors, assuring the benefits of the method were only being added to, never lessened. In most recent years, I've incorporated particular aspects to prepare clients for healthy connection to themselves and others. I have seen that gaining great freedom from processing trauma is the unlocking of a person's potential for healthy living. The connection perspective is essential for that freedom to lead to greater wholeness, and prevent potential problems. Without a connection perspective, greater freedom may be temporary, like unsticking the accelerator in a car, but having the steering fail. The person could drive faster, but still end up in a ditch. Incorporating the connection perspective is no great leap since disconnection is the essence of trauma.

The stories I share in these pages are my own experience of treatment and what I experienced providing the Neuro-Reformatting and Integration (NRI) method as I've honed it over the last decade. These examples were chosen because they illustrate particular points and proved over and over the efficacy of this treatment model. My hope is that in using these examples I can demystify trauma and the disconnection trauma causes. I want you to see that effective treatment, which treats the roots instead of symptoms, is possible when we work with the brain the way the brain actually works.

These stories, along with all of my experiences of working with the brave girls and boys, women and men I've had the honor of treating, keep me awake at night; once you understand trauma, its effects and how to treat it, you can't help but see needless suffering almost everywhere. Week in and week out, I've seen it give the folks with whom I've worked a sort of x-ray vision into themselves, others, relationships and afford so many a greater sense of freedom. Understanding breeds compassion, and compassion, be it for others or ourselves, is always a good thing.

As good as understanding is, the best news of all is that there is healing. I lived for 17 years in torment from chronic trauma and another 16 years in mind-melting frustration of trying to get help all while enduring more traumatic events, since trauma begets drama, which begets further trauma. Why was I in such excruciating emotional pain? Why didn't therapy help? Why didn't hospitalizations help? Why didn't medications help? Why didn't traditional talk therapy relieve the psychological pain? My years of therapy had produced more questions than answers. I cheated death on more than one occasion, but I spent a lot of time thinking about how good it would be to die. I know in my heart that if I hadn't received real relief when I did, I wouldn't have been around to write this.

What would you do if you woke up tomorrow with the cure for cancer? How would you get the word out? Who would believe you? Wouldn't you hurt for those who are senselessly hurting? As isolated as I felt in those years, I know I wasn't alone. I know there are other prisoners of that war who are not yet free. I want to get a message back to them. I want them to know the escape route. I want them to know they are not forgotten. For those waging personal wars now and those who will come in the future, I want you to benefit from all my lost years. May they make your journey shorter and smoother. In my seeking years, the books I came across would describe trauma for the first portion of the book and then describe coping in the second half. What I've experienced personally and professionally is that there is life beyond coping. There are so many survivor support groups, but there is more to life than surviving! I

9

know when you can barely tolerate the depression and anxiety, even coping and/or surviving sound too good to be true and, frankly, over the years, that's the objection I've most often heard. As expensive as medications, treatment or intensive treatment may be, the most expensive part is hope, just like it was for me.

Back in 2010, I did a five-show series for television on trauma and received about 300 phone calls and emails in response. I've been the guest on numerous radio shows and quoted as an expert in multiple books on trauma. The most consistent response from people has been a request for my book, but the request was baffling to me. I hadn't written a book. I said this method of treatment works. Why waste time reading a book? If you're suffering, just get treatment. Then, some months ago, I was sharing about one of the little preverbal children I discuss in this book with a social worker from Summit County Children Services in Akron, OH who has referred a great number of children to me over the years. She told me she hoped I was writing these things down because it would be a shame for them to be lost. That stopped me in my tracks. I had always seen how useful these examples are for illustrating points in training, but I had never considered there would come a time when I'm no longer training and even a day when I'm no longer alive and this knowledge would stop with me. "No, that can't happen!" I thought. What about all the people who could benefit from my suffering and my work in the field? I was a client for 16 years and have been a therapist for almost 12, at the time of writing this book. Perhaps that's why I see things from the client perspective first. What if I was the person needing help? What if the knowledge of how to help someone like me was suddenly gone? I understood. This information wasn't just for my use. I had to write.

As I practiced counseling, results like those in these pages became bittersweet to me. Week in and week out, I'd get feedback from the client of that week and those of weeks past about how wonderfully they were doing since treatment. For some, the results were immediate. For some, it was months down the road, like the young adult who seemed somewhat unimpressed at the end of the week of intensive, but emailed me some months later to tell me how NRI treatment had set her on a different trajectory of peace and potential in her life. She was unaware of the freedom that had been made available to her until she returned home and was reengaged in her life. As she began to go about her normal activities, she was able to exercise a much greater freedom. Of course, I am always delighted for each individual and their loved ones and filled with an ineffable sense of gratitude for the privilege of being a part of their journey, but I ache for the millions of others out there seeking healing with a sincere and determined heart. So many people are desperate to do whatever is necessary, but with no idea what that is.

Whether it's you or your loved one suffering, there is no trauma history too great and no experience too small. Treating clients such as veterans, a first responder from 9-11, and victims of Columbine all taught me it is not necessarily the headline events that make the headlines in our hearts. For example, a young man who had been on the front lines and seen hand-to-hand combat told me worse for him than battle was being verbally abused by his father when he was a little boy. He explained that when he joined the Army

11

he knew what he was signing up for. They gave him a gun, taught him how to use it, told him others were going to be trying to kill him, and to go defend himself. The situation had been drastically different when he was seven years old, alone, in his footie pajamas eating his cereal and getting verbally decimated by the man who was supposed to be his protector.

Whether you understand it intellectually by the term trauma, or you know it more personally as childhood, there is help that is not re-traumatizing. Many times in traditional therapy, I would be sent into a flashback. I felt like a toilet with a bad clog. Each week, the plunger would come out as the therapists would work away and just as the putrid waters were about to overflow all over the floor, the 50 minutes would be up and I'd be sent out until next week, when we would try the whole thing again. This is not that. When I went through ITR treatment, which I eventually honed into the model I use, it finally felt like the Roto-Rooter. The clog was gone. It is that evidence-based brief, effective method of recoding traumas I refined over the years to provide as much treatment as effectively as possible in as efficient a manner as possible, all the while with a view to preparing clients for engaging in relationships and life from a place of healthy connection to themselves and others.

A couple of years ago I attended a conference on the topic of trauma in Cleveland, OH. It promised to be groundbreaking information and the speaker was a major headliner in the field. I was ecstatic. I quickly set aside time in my schedule and made plans to attend. When I arrived at the hotel, I immediately saw the venue reserved for the event was quite large. Certainly, many mental health professionals had been as enthusiastic about this event as I was. As the talks began, I took a quick head count and estimated roughly 350+ attendees. I could only imagine how many clients we could reach over the course of our careers. How many therapists were attending because they were in the same spot Rachel had been trying to help me so many years ago?

As the hours went by, the predominant thrust of the speaker's message was that trauma is not really treatable in any profound way, any benefit took a tremendous amount of time to affect and the way to combat trauma biologically was mostly through tai chi and yoga. I was dumbfounded and distraught. What a bully pulpit he had and how many therapists had come to find out what to do for Susan, who really seemed like she couldn't endure another day, or Vince, who had already attempted suicide numerous times and wanted so desperately to find relief.

I writhed in my chair and began blowing up a colleague's phone with text messages. She knew how excited I had been to attend the conference and to hear someone else speak on the types of radical changes I was seeing in my own practice. I told her what the content actually was and how excruciating it was to think of all the people who were represented by the professionals in attendance and how drastically everything being taught flew in the face of what I'd experienced personally and seen as a practitioner first hand. She encouraged me to approach the presenter at a break. Being a researcher should certainly mean he was seeking truth and if someone else knew what I knew wouldn't I want them to share it with me? I ought to consider inviting him to lunch or dinner, she encouraged, it was really the only professional and charitable course of action.

Needless to say, I was highly intimidated to approach the internationally renowned presenter. My stomach was full of butterflies the size of pterodactyls, but I decided I had a duty to those in attendance at this conference and all those who might hear him speak in the future and the clients of all the clinicians represented. At the next break, I called on all my courage, gulped hard and approached the stage, which was taller than I. Since he didn't leave the stage to speak with those who approached, I stood lower than his shoe and told him I would like the chance to talk to him about the types of things I was seeing in my practice. Not long before I had seen someone's life saved through the physical side benefit of treatment. He sneered, scoffed, closed his eyes and looked away saying, "What's so different about what you're doing?" Before I had a chance to answer, he closed his eyes, turned his head, scoffed again and waved me away like he was shooing a fly.

I was incredulous to find someone who was supposed to be seeking the best care possible for hurting people wouldn't be open to hearing about something helpful. It was true he didn't know me, but we were all professionals. Weren't we all on the same team? How could we let our own biases get in the way of helping hurting people? I'm not sure why he couldn't hear me that day, but I knew there were others who had asked in their own hearts if there wasn't more and they were willing to listen.

Since there are only so many people I can treat in a lifetime, I knew this treatment must spread beyond me. Over the years, people

14

came to me from around the country and many from outside of the United States. The effort people would show in availing themselves of treatment, like the young adult who came 70 hours by bus, was immensely edifying. My desire is to make this treatment known and available.

The myriad effects of trauma: emotional, cognitive, physical, and relational, are crippling. When we come into the world, all we really have that is uniquely ours is our God-given potential. If it can be stolen through adversity, then that would be tragically sad, but that does not have to be the end of the story. Untreated trauma leads to people being on disability or underproductive, and the societal effects are those of addiction, unintended pregnancies, and violence. The socio-economic ramifications are bankrupting our nation. We are all impacted in so many areas, even if we haven't personally suffered traumas or have been able to continue to function daily. Effective treatment can help to revolutionize our world where trauma is an unspoken epidemic.

Many people suffering from trauma are unaware of how it is blocking their personal growth and ability to maximize their potential, find peace, and for that to flow out into their relationships. There is some fantastic work out there on how to grow personally, but sadly, most of it doesn't take into account the way trauma holds us captive to lies, pain and a life of fighting ghosts in our everyday lives. If you've tried to pursue personal growth for yourself and have been discouraged and bewildered that the beauty and freedom described don't seem to apply to you, know that is a lie. Join the resistance. Spread the word. There is more to life than surviving. We were all born to THRIVE!

.

3

Overcoming Aunt Betsy

Over the years people have asked me how to know if a particular experience needs to be addressed through this treatment. I share with them what I've experienced myself. I've come to see it as the difference in thinking about an experience verses feeling an experience. If the emotions remain present, if an emotion has me instead of me having the emotion, then I know that I need to apply the NRI process to an event. Another way I've come to recognize the need to address an issue is if it seems somewhat stuck in my mind in snapshots of the experience itself. Those events often seem to find resolution once the impacting traumas have been adequately addressed.

Over the past 14 years since treatment, various incidents have come to mind, and it has been obvious they needed to be processed. When that happened, I again sought treatment. If you're wondering why I couldn't do my own treatment, it's because that would be like a right-handed hand surgeon performing surgery on his own right thumb. Hopefully, this will become clear to you as I get into the explanation of how trauma and the biology of the brain are interwoven. My consistent results through the years have thoroughly convinced me of the effectiveness of this treatment. I am so sure of it that if treatment didn't seem to work, I would question what it was I had missed and still needed to address rather than questioning the method. Each time, I was amazed at how consistently effective it was. That's not to say that the last 14 years have been uneventful. After having gone through intensive treatment, there was a tremendous amount of integration and post-treatment growth that was finally available to me that had previously been blocked by the traumatic experiences. For example, I had lived in crisis for so long that I had to learn how to become accustomed to being peaceful. That might sound strange, but it required a shift both emotionally and physically. I've dedicated myself to maximizing that integration. I believe as long as we live, there is always more room for growth, and I find that both hopeful and exciting.

One such experience had delayed my ability to write this book. For the last 10 years I have toyed with the idea of recording the cases we'll soon unpack here. I have started and restarted manuscripts only to abandon them. I just felt like I was trying to push a boulder up a steep hill. I had a definite mental block about writing. It felt like an insurmountable obstacle. Finally, I found help by processing an event from over 30 years ago. Though there wasn't intense emotion connected to it, it would come to mind every time I was blocked in writing. Finally, it occurred to me to apply this method of treatment to it, as well.

When I was a freshman in high school, I was selected to participate in an Advanced Placement English class. In the context of my childhood, it was one of the only times I felt recognized for doing something outstanding. When my senior year of high school arrived, the entire year was preparation to take the College Level Equivalency Program, also known as the CLEP test. A high grade on the test could exempt me from the requirement of freshman English in college. A superb grade guaranteed the exemption. More importantly, my English teacher, Miss Murphy, was an amazing lady. She had a huge heart and was truly devoted to us. We were more than just students. She truly invested in each one of us. It was obvious she cared at a point in my life when I felt no one else did. I so much wanted to perform well to express my gratitude to her, but the strife with which my senior year was wrought made it virtually impossible to attend to my studies. Each week or so, our class was required to read another novel or two. It was a huge struggle given my circumstances, yet somehow what I was able to glean from class discussions allowed me to surmise enough to perform well on the timed writings we were assigned.

The only book I had read from cover to cover was *The Night Thoreau Spent in Jail* by Robert E. Lee and Jerome Lawrence. It was about Thoreau taking a stand for what he believed in regardless of the cost. I related closely to it because of my circumstances at the time. I devoured that book voraciously. When it came time to take the CLEP test, the writing section was on the topic of civil disobedience. I could not believe my eyes. I was profoundly relieved. I wrote with passion and ease.

Some weeks later, my CLEP test results were in, and my father drove me to get them. On the way, I explained to him what the test was and that the grading scale was a zero to five with five being the best and guaranteeing the ability to be exempt from freshman English in college. Once retrieving my results, I returned to the car to open them. As I did, my eyes fell on the five in the right hand column. I had to blink and double-check that. Oh my goodness! What a way to let Miss Murphy see the impact of her investment in me!

Then, my father sighed and spoke, "What did you get?"

"A five", I replied.

He shook his head, "You're gonna have to tell your Aunt Betsy. It'll only be worse if she finds out some other way." Neither of us knew what her response would be. We only knew it wouldn't be good.

Aunt Betsy, not an actual blood relative, was an older lady who had inaugurated herself as our aunt. Somehow, what she said always seemed so impacting, but she could be highly critical, and she often behaved as though she was in competition with me. Though I knew she'd pry the information out if I didn't tell her, it wasn't a task I was excited to complete and so I decided to delay it. At school the next day, I learned I was the only one who had received the highest mark, which doubled my joy and pride. It made it that much more meaningful to me because if I hadn't received that score, Miss Murphy would have had no one who did.

Within a few days, Aunt Betsy dropped by, I decided to take the opportunity to get it over with and communicate the news. I tried to downplay it as much as possible.

"Oh, I got the results from that test," I said simply and without excitement.

"What did you get?" she inquired.

Ok, I can still make this seem like no big deal, I thought. "A five", came my response. I reasoned that without knowing the grading scale, a five would seem like a low score and, somehow bad was preferable and would allow me to fly under the radar, but she pushed for more detail.

"So, what was the grading scale?" she asked.

"Zero to five," I replied, again giving as little information as possible.

"So, a five is the best?" she continued.

"Yes, Ma'am," I answered.

"How many other kids got fives?" she questioned further.

"No one", I reluctantly replied.

After a long pause, came, "Well, what do you want us to do, bow down and swing incense?"

I was silent. The message was clear. The meaning behind those words was, 'who do you think you are?' The meaning would come back every time I would attempt to write a book and every time I would consider these cases I've laid out here and not just these, but those of the vast majority of people with whom I've had the privilege to work. The powerful results available with the necessary work made me cringe. I had been programmed that good results were nothing to celebrate and discussing them was a sign of arrogance and could be used as ammunition against me. Once I received treatment for that painful experience, it was no longer an

21

impediment to writing. I was able to finally feel compassion for the 17-year-old part of me and yet not feel locked in the takeaway message that being knowledgeable on a topic is bad. The feeling after this type of trauma treatment is not like what we are used to experiencing in our consumer society. When you go to the store and buy a pair of shoes you've really been wanting or get tickets to a concert you're excited to attend, the feeling is that something has been acquired. The result of treatment is typically the feeling that something has been removed, like a splinter or like what was once a wall is now a door, as one client described it.

Aunt Betsy's comment wasn't something that caused flashbacks or nightmares, and the memory itself felt very distant to me, but the message had still been internalized and the damage done. As a therapist, I believe it's my duty to continue to do my own emotional work. I know when clients come for treatment they're expecting our best. I don't believe we can lead anyone to wholeness greater than our own. The advantage of staying on top of our personal growth is that we can be in tune with what is driving us. Because of this, I was open to the awareness of this memory in the back of my mind when trying to write. I admit I delayed addressing it. I had many of the same reasons I hear from clients. Was it that big of a deal? Wasn't 30 years a long time ago? Could it really be blocking me? Anyway, I was functioning just fine. Despite all my delays in doing my own work, the change since processing it is undeniable. What's in your way of becoming the best version of you?

Week in and week out, I've been asked why the method was not more widespread and used more often. There are a few reasons. First of all, as I've mentioned, it requires a great deal of hope. Most often people suffering from trauma have concluded there is something fundamentally wrong with them. To believe there could be hope for a life beyond coping is just too great a stretch. Secondly, intensive outpatient for individuals doesn't fit into any of the procedure codes of insurance companies and so it has been an out-of-pocket expense for most people, with state funded, post-adoptive subsidies covering services at times or, at other times, funding through a state's victim's assistance program. Finally, there is a lack of client education. There is an enormous need for clients and their loved ones to better understand trauma and its far-reaching tentacles and the treatment available.

My journey had been long and fruitless. Trying to attend school had been grueling and yet I could see no other way. At one point, my therapist and doctor had even wanted me to undergo electroconvulsive shock therapy (ECT) because the depression was so deep and unrelenting, but I would not submit because they were unable to explain to me how it works. I only have one brain and without a logical rationale, I wasn't willing to subject it to something that seemed little more than a shot in the dark. Due to the level of desperation I had experienced and the great extent to which I was helped, I was completely convinced of this method of treatment's efficacy. Once I began practicing, that level of confidence was a great gift and has only increased as I've witnessed the benefit others have experienced.

Additionally, suffering so deeply for so long motivates me to get the greatest benefit for people. Shortly after beginning practice, I was reprimanded by a director for "getting people better too quickly." She told me it made her feel like I thought she was a bad therapist. I was shocked. Aren't we all supposed to be working together for the purpose of relieving the suffering of others as quickly as possible? Had egos like these prevented others and me from being helped more quickly? All the time I spent in emotional pain has driven me to want people to receive the most effective help in as timely a fashion as possible.

4

Making Trauma History

Neuro-Reformatting and Integration is usually one week, on occasion up to two weeks of reformatting memory files and getting equipped for the future. Though that requires a chunk of time away from school or work, the results can be remarkable. A common concern of people prior to treatment is that the intensity of the emotions of the traumas will be present again, but this method is designed to prevent that from happening. Though the content can surely be difficult, the retelling is managed in such a way as to limit the impact on the client. Completing treatment within a week or two is often the gentlest way to provide effective trauma help. Once there is a way to truly release the traumatic memories, it seems the brain wants nothing more than to get that done. Intensive treatment allows clients to roll up their sleeves and plow through the past in order to finally live in the here and now and move into the future in freedom.

In the beginning of my practice, I tried to provide this method in hourly sessions once a week. It was a frustrating experience. Though I knew the treatment could be used in that way, it flew in the face of how we're wired as human beings. It's typical to come in for a weekly therapy session and discuss the difficulties of life since the time of the last session. Doing so at the beginning usually took at least 10 minutes and making sure the client was in a good spot to leave took another several minutes at the end. The time left was not sufficient to completely process a trauma and usually extended the process of working through one event to a month for an adult and maybe two weeks for a child. Most people don't have one or two traumas to process. The time required for treatment in a non-intensive format greatly increases the amount of time needed. Unfortunately, the lack of processing delays any real benefit for so long most people end up not following through with treatment. I decided it was better to keep the application of the method to an intensive format since trying to make it fit an insurance code stood to compromise the benefit. The NRI method can be used in the hourly session format most clinicians provide, but some specific strategies should be implemented in order to take care of all the client's clinical needs.

Traditional counseling addresses issues as seen in the two outer circles on Figure 1. Oftentimes, behavior is the focus of treatment. Traumatized clients are usually left white-knuckling it, and not able to hit the mark. Remember the traumatized person is functioning today with emotions from traumas of the past. They are operating in the emotional part of the brain and many times not on the level of conscious awareness, but instead as a result of a feeling that situations are a matter of life and death. Usually, thinking through or talking about the trauma is made the focus of most counseling, but the intellect cannot override those trauma messages.

We can end up knowing what to do, but having no idea how to do it. When traumatic experiences are processed, the change is able to flow out from within the person.

Figure 1 – Treating Trauma at the Root

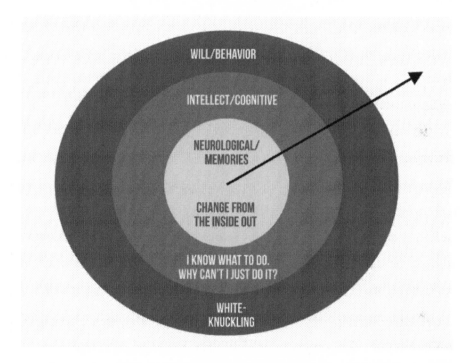

Since it takes a great deal of education and training to master this method of treatment, I won't go into the specifics. My concern is people may try to process their own traumas and muddy the waters for effective work that would eventually be needed with a trained NRI therapist. Because I can easily and succinctly describe what is done, the model can sound simple. What is far too complicated to outline here is all the rationale behind each component, along with what happens in special situations. If you are a clinician who is reading this and you are interested in training, please go to my website and learn how to get involved.

The NRI model of treatment borrows from the ITR model in that it uses directed art or play therapy to reformat the memories so they are finally experienced like they are in the past. Though art and play therapy are both typically rather open-ended and unstructured, in this model they are systematically and strategically used. They help to access the traumatic memory material, since it is encoded through the right/more creative hemisphere of the brain. The therapist helps the process along to make sure the information isn't merely an expression of the traumatic events, but a re-coding of them the way the left hemisphere of the brain needs. Because the left side of the brain can differentiate between past, present and future, this recoding allows the painful emotions of the traumatic events to be experienced as something that is no longer taking place.

The memory reformatting and the integration components are equally important and treatment would be lacking without both. The trauma processing is necessary to unshackle us from the past and the connection component is necessary for freedom in the present and the ability to move forward in the future. The integration work helps the client to connect the part of themselves that has intellectually known the trauma was over and the part of themselves that has persisted with all the emotions and negative messages. This allows the emotional part to finally experience a sense of safety and the ability to be present to the here and now. This is a key component. Trauma clients are typically left feeling broken and fundamentally flawed in the wake of horrible events. It's not enough for the event to be experienced as past. Through the NRI process, the person comes to discover the truth of who they are rather than the lies they absorbed through the traumatic experiences. That self-knowledge allows the opportunity for self-acceptance, and it is from connection to self that a person can healthily connect to others.

5

How Trauma Works

Over the years, I've come to see NRI treatment like physical therapy for the brain. It works to reformat how memories are encoded so the emotions of the traumas are finally experienced as past rather than current. Oftentimes, there are many side benefits I never could have expected or predicted.

The truth is, we are body, mind and spirit and the more we take care of all three of those aspects of ourselves, the more health and wholeness we'll have. It doesn't make sense to lie around eating junk food all day and pray for our cholesterol to lower, just like it doesn't make sense to pursue mental health, but not take care of our bodies. Those three dimensions of us are interwoven. If a person eats more sugar than their system can handle, of course they could have serious impulse control issues, just like if someone doesn't exercise, what sort of message are they sending themselves about their own worth? To be whole, we have to pursue health in all areas.

Of course, life is not always an ideal experience of connection and is sometimes, quite painful. For all the many years I was in treatment, I wondered if I was weak, a wimp or had too much self-pity. I thought if I could toughen up and not be so sensitive, then the neglect and abuse would no longer be a problem. I thought it was my way of looking at it that made it a problem. Over the years, many people told me they thought the same way about themselves. It's not true. In order to understand why traumatizing events can continue to affect us long after they are over, we need to understand some biology.

The brain has two hemispheres, right and left, and an area in the middle called the corpus callosum that connects the two sides. See Figure 2. This is a simplistic representation of the tasks the two sides are more closely responsible for since most of what we do requires both sides working together in a coordinated way. Without needing to all become neurologists, we can use this basic model to gain insight into life, experience and behavior. The left hemisphere has the strengths you see listed. It helps us do logic and reasoning. It likes order and for events to be sequential. We have two verbal areas of the brain that are both in the left hemisphere. Quite relevant, also, is that the left hemisphere knows the difference in past, present and future. If we are going to communicate something to someone in a left-brain mode, those are the 'apps' we have at our disposal. Therefore, the communication tends to be in words that logically describe the situation and when it took place. Those words flow together and make sense. This is, of course, easier to do when what we are describing is not emotionally charged. If I asked you to tell me about the last time you went to the grocery store, as long as it wasn't a traumatic experience, you could most likely do so quite succinctly and it wouldn't feel like there was more to convey that you just couldn't articulate.

Figure 2 - Healthy Brain Function.

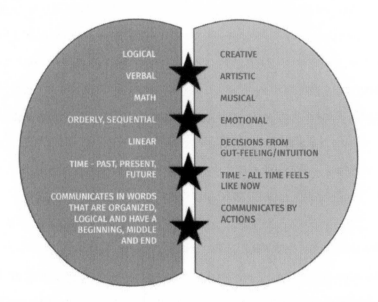

However, if the experience you were describing to me was quite distressing, doing so would most likely be much different. That's because the right side of the brain is the side through which the traumatic event would have become encoded and the right side operates with a vastly different set of abilities. The right side is the more creative and artistic part. Because it is the most closely connected to the limbic system (the emotional center of the brain), it is more emotional. As opposed to making decisions rooted in logic, like the left side naturally would, the right side would go more off gut feeling or intuition. The right side experiences all time like the present. That's why decades after a traumatic event, that very event may continue to be experienced as though it is still taking place. The emotions may be just as raw or intense as when the event first happened. The old adage, 'time heals all wounds,' simply isn't true. Sadly, many people wait great lengths of time after traumatic events, hoping to spontaneously feel better, but trauma is more like a large splinter in your hand. If you don't get it out, the wound will fester and become irritated and perhaps even infected. Even if your skin did heal up around or over the splinter, you'd certainly become acutely aware of the pain when you used your hand, even years later once you'd forgotten about ever getting that splinter in the first place.

As the days, and years go by and emotional pain persists, we take on mistaken messages. Many people begin to believe they are broken and incapable. Many suffering children get labeled as bad kids. Without any verbal areas in the right hemisphere, we tend to communicate emotions by our actions. For example, how do you imagine you would respond if someone told you you won the lottery? I certainly imagine my eyes would widen and I'd become intensely excited and smile, and though incredulous at first, once I knew it was true, I imagine I'd laugh and jump around like a little kid. I wouldn't be consciously choosing to do any of those things. In ways like this, we act out emotion without words and without intention. The same doesn't go so well when the emotions are those of anger, hurt, shame, or the like. Those actions can be profoundly misunderstood, even by the persons themselves and are often misconstrued as proof that the person is bad or broken.

In non-traumatic events, the two hemispheres work together beautifully and are quite complimentary. They have strengths that help each other, like a great relationship. Both sides have exquisite types of intelligence, which are equal in value and yet quite different. Without the left hemisphere, we may be so emotional that we'd be driven only by our desires and never have the discipline we need to accomplish great feats or to tend to our responsibilities, but without the right side, we may be like Mr. Spock in *Star Trek* and devoid of the capacity for compassion and empathy. The brain has no smarter side or better side, no unintelligent or bad side.

Trauma-Compromised Brain Function

When trauma occurs, the two sides don't function together in harmony. Instead, the stress hormones released cause the left hemisphere to constrict, thus the event becomes encoded through the right hemisphere. The right side is the most closely wired to the emotional center of the brain. If someone is acting like they're not in their right mind, it may very well be because they're in their right brain, meaning a full understanding of the emotion they're experiencing may be contained in their past experiences. Remembering this can help us have compassion for people when their behavior may otherwise be frightening, frustrating or hurtful. Again, understanding breeds compassion.

34

One of the parts of the emotional center is the amygdala shown in Figure 3. It is responsible for fear learning. In teaching kids about the amygdala, a colleague refers to this portion of the brain as Amy G. Dala (amygdala) when he's educating kids about brain function. Amy, you see, has a tendency to be fearful, but fear learning is actually very necessary. What would it be like if crossing a street or touching a hot burner required slow deliberation and careful consideration each time?

Figure 3 - Cross-section of Brain

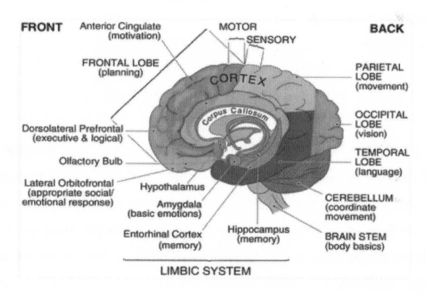

We need those types of instinctual and automatic responses for our very survival. Unfortunately, in the case of trauma, because the event is encoded through the right hemisphere, it continues to be experienced like it's NOW and any of the things we perceived or experienced during the original event can later send the alarm system into overdrive, even without our conscious awareness. Let's say I'm out driving on a warm, bright, sunny day with *Hello* by Adele on the radio and the smell of coffee in my Jeep and someone in a blue truck who is driving erratically suddenly runs me off the road. Any of those facts, the song, the sunshine and warmth, the smell of coffee, even feeling happy, trucks, the color blue, could become like landmines because my amygdala could tell me they are potentially threatening or even deadly, due to what it learned to fear. None of those is life threatening. In the case of trauma, we're left with broad generalizations we didn't consciously choose and of which we may not even be aware.

Let's say it's years later and I'm out driving and have passed by someone in a blue truck who is driving a little fast. I might even have a cup of coffee in my car. The proverbial bell in my amygdala could go off without my conscious awareness. I may have been feeling really great and all of a sudden have been filled with a sense of anxiety or have been sent into a panic attack. I may not be able to connect the dots to the memory from so many years earlier, nevertheless, I'd be left wondering what was wrong with me and feeling fragile because an enjoyable experience so easily turned sour for no conscious reason. Now, multiply this by six or eight or 20 traumatic events all of which may plant many more landmines in my amygdala. Though it makes perfect sense that a person may end up feeling anxious and depressed, broken and inadequate, it is, at the same time, the furthest thing from the truth. Those responses would be happening because the brain is doing what it is wired to do, which means it's functioning well. In this way, trauma symptoms are a cause for hope.

The term post-traumatic stress disorder is a misnomer. It would be much more accurate to call it post-traumatic event disorder. Anyone who has ever suffered the ongoing effects of trauma knows the traumatic stress is not over! Therein lies the crux of the problem. When you look at the cross-section of the brain in Figure 3, notice how close the limbic system is to the brain stem. How much does your conscious, intentional thought control your pulse or digestion? It doesn't. That's how little control we have over the landmines trauma sets up in the amygdala that are in turn triggered by everyday occurrences. It's not a matter of weakness or over-sensitivity any more than lack of diligence can be blamed for heartburn. The limbic system responds to a reminder of a traumatic event 25 times faster than the neocortex. Our sense of fear is triggered much faster than our ability to reason can get on board. There's no way we can control our automatic response to something when it doesn't reach our conscious awareness. From a survival perspective, this makes us finely attuned to those things that have previously been sources of danger. This intense sensitivity can help us live to fight another day, but feeling like we are fighting the remainder of our days gets old fast.

It's for these reasons that trauma causes so darn many symptoms in so many areas. Think of the typical types of emotions we experience when we go through a difficult or painful event. Some, which come readily to mind, are fear, terror, powerlessness, helplessness, anger, rage, humiliation, shame, rejection, abandonment and that's just for starters. We're left open to re-experiencing any or all of those things when the trigger to the landmines in the amygdala gets tripped and possibly without our awareness that it did. This makes it so elusive for folks to identify trauma as the root cause of suffering. Many times people are misdiagnosed because the vast majority of clinicians don't have adequate training in trauma. As clinicians, we are trained to diagnose based on symptoms rather than the less visible roots of symptoms. Unfortunately, the focus is on making particular symptoms go away rather than treating the roots. If I get rid of a section of vine in my yard, it may grow twice as quickly in another direction. If I pull up the root, the vine is gone.

Given how biologically-oriented trauma is, I believe that in the coming years all mental health workers will be required to have training in a certain amount of neuroscience. In my 16 years of therapy as a client, I don't know how many times I was asked, in reference to some painful event, "How does that make you feel?" I remember being consistently incredulous and thinking that if the therapist had to ask how abuse made me feel, maybe they should find a different line of work. I wondered why they believed telling the stories again and again would magically help me feel better? Regardless of how many times I answered that question over those years, it never made me feel any differently because the traumas were still encoded in the same way, leaving them experienced as current events. The landmines were still as sensitive to being tripped, but I left the sessions feeling the additional pressure to somehow be "over it". I didn't know there was treatment that could help on a biological level. The truth is we don't need to repeatedly talk about how events made us feel. Once they are physically reformatted and experienced as part of the past, the emotions are *experienced* as past, as well. NRI treatment can help make your traumas history. Let's take a look at a couple of striking cases of how biologically based trauma is.

6

Freedom from Trauma Messages

For the next two cases, take a look at Figure 4 and consider that the takeaway messages from traumas become the lenses through which we see ourselves, relate to others and interact with our environment. It's one thing to hear that as a simple learning point. It's quite another when it has skin and bones.

Figure 4 - Trauma-Compromised Brain Function

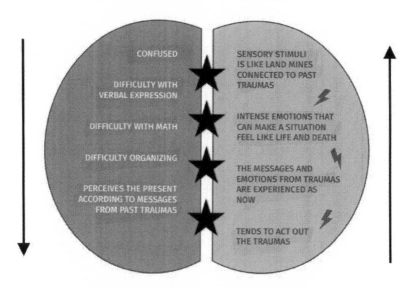

Anne was a very bright, high-functioning woman who came to see me. We had worked for the better portion of our allotted time and ended up finishing treatment of the traumas on the list we had made prior to her arrival. Since we had a little time left, I reassessed her list with her to see if, perchance, she was overlooking anything. She said there wasn't anything she could think of, so I explored a little further. I mentioned that oftentimes adults have been through some sort of accident and can tend to forget to mention. She told me there was one, but it "wasn't a big deal." I asked her what had happened. The following is what she shared.

Decades before, she had a job as a guest liaison for a company. They happened to be putting up new construction and she was in charge of showing guests around the construction site. There was a road going around the construction site that the construction vehicles were prohibited from using. So, while driving on that road, she had every expectation of safety. She had guests in her car both in the back seat and passenger seat. The vehicle was a stick shift and she had put it into neutral while she sat turned facing her guests and describing to them what was being built. Suddenly she saw a look of terror on the face of one of the ladies in the back seat. When she turned back to the front to see what the woman was frightened by, she saw an enormous construction vehicle called a land mover. The wheels were larger than her car. That piece of equipment was backing up towards her vehicle on the very road it wasn't supposed to use. She quickly moved to put the car in reverse. As she hit the accelerator, so she could quickly back out of the way, the engine flooded, and the car stalled out.

She was very conscientious and felt responsible for the guests and vehicle and told the others to get out of the car and to safety. They did, and she continued to attempt to restart the car, but all the while, the land mover headed directly for her. The cab was so high the construction worker couldn't see her automobile down below. Finally, when that gigantic construction vehicle came across the hood of her car, she decided to abandon ship herself, but it was too late. In crushing the hood, the frame of the car was damaged and so the door would not open. She was trapped in her vehicle while it was being crushed. She even lunged into the back seat just to try to gain some distance, though very little, from the land mover.

As she told me this, I found myself on the edge of my seat wondering what happened. I was surprised she had told me this event was insignificant. I told her it sounded like a near-death experience to me. She said that in reconsidering it, it was scary and she had even lost control of her bowels. She also had gone into shock and wasn't able to regulate her body temperature.

Thankfully, the guests who had evacuated the car had thrown handfuls of gravel at the cab and were able to get the attention of the driver. He had stopped just in time before crushing her in her car. Even though she had no visible injury, there had been an emotional effect of which she was unaware. As we processed this event, she sat back and said, under her breath, in amazed realization, "Oh my gosh! That's why!" Of course I inquired, "That's why what?" She shared with me that she traveled frequently and regardless of the fact that she was very bright and intelligent, if the vehicles in front of her either slowed, as they may fluctuate their rate of speed on the road, or began to back up towards her, as may happen in a parking lot, she was compelled to jump out of the car. Many times, as it turned out, her husband had to drive with one hand in front of her, to prevent her from reaching for the door handle. This would happen even if they were driving 70 miles per hour on the highway.

Of course, she knew she was safer inside her vehicle than she would be by leaping into traffic at high speed. She knew that in her neocortex, that is, but that terribly traumatic accident decades prior had programmed her amygdala with the message that being in such typical situations was actually a matter of life and death situation. Therefore, when she encountered events reminiscent of the accident, her amygdala pulled the fire alarm and sent her the 'GET OUT OF THE CAR NOW!' message. What she had concluded she should have done in that experience so long ago became hard-wired into subsequent experiences reminiscent of it. What might have been a good idea in that instance many years prior wasn't always a safe idea in new situations. She needed the mental flexibility to take into account the specifics of each new situation and tailor her responses accordingly. For Anne and for each of us, trauma hardwiring doesn't allow for the incorporation of new information and nuanced responses.

Over the years, many people have come for treatment already knowing where their mixed-up messages came from. It wasn't her realization of this fact that brought her freedom, because, as it turns out, her compulsion to jump out of vehicles ended that day. What affected the relief was that her brain finally, through treatment, came to *experience* the event like it was in the past and freed her up to experience life without that trauma filter. It is for this same reason that treatment with a preverbal child can be highly effective. We aren't relying on their ability to reason with new insights. It is defusing the landmines in the amygdala that brings the relief of trauma symptoms.

Another case much like this was that of Cassie, a woman in her mid-30s, who came to me one day. Since she was wearing short sleeves, I could see her arms were covered with scars. She struggled terribly against the compulsion to cut herself. She told me she had tried every type of counseling imaginable along with hypnosis and even acupuncture, but she still couldn't fight the urge to injure herself. She had numerous reasons for not wanting to cut. She told me that she had no medical training and feared she may accidentally cut an artery and kill herself and she wasn't trying to die. Cassie was a Christian and told me she believed her body was a temple of the

Holy Spirit and she didn't want to desecrate that temple. She also knew it wasn't emotionally healthy for her to injure herself. She had been injured, as it turns out, so much in her past and she didn't want to treat herself in the same terrible ways she had been treated. The nature of the cutting had even taken a rather macabre tone that was quite disturbing, and I didn't really know what to make of it. It seems she would awaken each morning with a number in her head and that was the number of ounces of blood she was compelled to bleed out of herself for that day. Thus, the people in her church had become quite frightened and had wanted to do deliverance prayer with her.

She asked me if I would be able to help her, and I said I believed I could. Over the years I had come to realize the mystery of the behavior is in the trauma history and that through processing the significant known traumas we could unlock the door to freedom. So, I gathered her trauma history, and we set to work. There was an interesting event on her list. It was strange to me because she said it was the only time she ever remembered her biological father being helpful. He was intensely cruel and abusive in his behavior towards her and when he would fight with her mother, he abused her as a way of retaliation against her mother. I wondered why, if he had been helpful in a situation, the event would have been traumatic. Nevertheless, one of my counseling professors used to say we may be experts on mental health, but the clients are the experts on themselves. Because of my own past encounters with not being heard by mental health professionals, I took those words to heart.

Though it didn't really make sense to me, we started to process the story that unfolded like this: She had been a little three year-old and was sitting by the coffee table in their living room one day. She was playing with toys when suddenly she heard angry voices in the kitchen, as her parents argued. Her father left the kitchen and went into the living room where little Cassie was. He picked her up and slammed her down into the coffee table, causing a large gash in her forehead. She began to bleed profusely, as head wounds do. As that little girl bled so much, he grabbed a towel and started applying pressure to the wound and began being what her little three-year-old eyes had perceived as 'nice' toward her mother. They rushed her to the hospital and, presumably made up some lie about how she had been injured. Nonetheless, she was treated and stitched, and they all went for ice cream.

From an adult perspective, one can see he hadn't been sincerely helpful. It's not a stretch to imagine that his helpfulness was a desperate attempt to suck up to her mother to avoid being reported to the authorities, but she hadn't been an adult. She had been a very young child. She was stuck living out of the lesson she had internalized at the time the event had occurred. As we processed the story, I could see what had happened and through the course of processing the event, she came to the realization on her own. As we did further work with the story, her eyes widened and her jaw dropped. She slumped back in her chair, as she was able to see the event for what it really was. She now had the perspective on the event as an adult. Her brain had quickly connected the dots and she understood that her three-year-old takeaway from the abusive event

46

was that once she bled, everything was ok, her daddy was helpful and mommy and daddy worked together to get her help and they had even gone for ice cream together as a family. As she shared her insight with me, she connected another point to her behavior of cutting. What she hadn't previously told me was that every morning she woke up with renewed resolve not to cut herself, but she wasn't able to actually stop because she was riddled with anxiety until she was injured. Her brain had, through that trauma, been programmed with the message that when she bled, everything would be ok and she would be safe.

Over two decades later, she still had that programming in her mind, despite years of therapy. Because thought work is a more superficial level than work on a biological level. She needed those events to be neurologically re-worked and experienced as past events to allow her to form a new perspective and gain freedom. The limbic system was driving Cassie, just the way Anne's had driven her. In the same way, she became free to experience the present rather than the past.

Preverbal Traumas

When we first come into the world, the left and right side of the brain are functioning pretty independently of each other. This is easy to see when trying to hand a baby a rattle or a bottle. The two tiny hands and arms aren't able to work together. Our original state is that the two halves of the brain operate as co-leaders, until a developmental change takes place in the brain once the two sides of the body are forced to work together in a coordinated way. Typically, that initial event is crawling. The corpus callosum is stimulated to myelinate. Myelin is the covering of the nerves that allows them to communicate electrically. It is this development that allows the two hemispheres to communicate and work together.

Such development continues up through around age three. Think of how much more uncoordinated little babies look than do children who can walk. Essentially, before the age of three, the bridge within the brain is out. This has a tremendous impact on how traumatic events are recalled. After three, we are much more likely to be able to recount a traumatic event. Most people say they don't remember anything before that age, but that's not true. For a fascinating TED Talk on the topic, check out, *What We Learn Before We're Born* by Annie Murphy Paul. She discusses how studies prove we even remember things that took place while we were in the womb. The difference is the things prior to age three, most of us can't recall. Let's distinguish between remembering and recalling. At the time an event happens, the brain encodes it, that is, remembers it. When we pull that memory back up is when we recall it. The traumatic events prior to three years of age are not typically recalled in a verbal way. The bridge wasn't built, or corpus callosum myelinated, and so we couldn't put words on the experience. Instead, the brain and rest of the body remembered it, in a visceral way.

Around the age of three, our world becomes full of words. Perhaps before that we might have sort of grunted and pointed. Maybe adults asked us a lot of yes/no questions and we could simply shake our heads to answer. After three, we usually develop a lot more verbal fluency that only increases from that point. Once we're school age and especially as adults, the world is mostly full of words from the time we awaken until when we go to bed at night. The left hemisphere of the brain was originally the co-leader. Once we're older, it's forced to lead for the majority of the day, since it's the side with the verbal and reasoning areas. When we get tired, stressed out, sick or rundown, it becomes a lot more difficult for that side to be the fake boss. It's not just more difficult to articulate things well at those times, but also to be logical, reasonable and do good problem solving. This is why sitting down with your spouse to work on the budget at midnight is not usually very successful. It's also the same reason 12-Step programs like Alcoholics Anonymous have the H.A.L.T. acronym. It stands as a reminder to not get too Hungry, Angry, Lonely or Tired, since it's harder to make the best, logical choices at those times.

7

Emotions, Connection, & Power

A couple of years ago I realized that despite all my graduate and post-graduate education, I had never been taught what emotions are. Oh, sure, I could name them; happy, sad, scared, angry, worried, confused and so on, but I had never been taught what purpose they serve. We have them from the moment we come into the world and even before, according to scientific research. The purpose of a nose, ears, eyes, skin, mouth and the other parts of us are easily discernible. It occurred to me that emotions, like our five senses, are sources of information.

Several years ago I had pain on the left side of my lower back. At the time I was working at a doctor's office. Neither the general practitioner, nor his two nurse practitioners, nor his nurse were able to help me figure out the source of the pain. When I first complained of it they suspected it might be a kidney stone and took an x-ray of the area, but there was no stone. Each day they continued to ask me where exactly the pain was, and each day I showed them. After three days, I woke up around one in the morning with the same pain, but it was radiating around to my abdomen. I thought I better go to the emergency room to get more diagnostic information. I feared, not being a medical professional, I could be missing important clues to something serious.

After many hours at the hospital, the tests came back showing nothing. The doctor came into the area where I had been waiting for the last two hours and asked me if I wanted narcotics. Narcotics? No! I didn't want to mask the pain. I wanted to know what it meant and if I simply numbed it away, I would have no access to that information. Surely it meant something. Whether we experience physical pleasure or pain, there is a cause. It isn't arbitrary. I wanted to know what it meant so I could find out what to do about it.

The next day, I went to my chiropractor. I hadn't yet realized how knowledgeable he is and so when I was being put in a treatment room, I only mentioned a problem with my shoulder that had been injured in a car accident. As the assistant left the room, I asked her to turn off the light so I could nap while I waited to be seen. I explained that I'd had very little sleep the night before because I had been in the emergency room. She happened to jot that in my chart. When the doctor entered the room, he turned on the light and immediately announced that the pain was from my psoas nerve. He knew exactly where it was. He didn't ask me to show him. Instead, he actually showed me. I was shocked. He explained how it made sense since I was working at a doctor's office. He told me the psoas nerve is often irritated by repetitive turning and twisting like he imagined I was doing a great deal of at work, as I was turning from charts to the copier to the phone to the fax to the window all day long. He was right, and he fixed it quickly and painlessly. I learned to report symptoms to him before I went to the emergency room.

That pain was information. Emotions, too, are information. Happiness tells me to be grateful. Anger usually indicates that a boundary has been crossed. Sadness lets me know there is a loss to grieve. Suspicion is usually my bullshit meter being activated. We tend to fear what we don't understand and, not knowing what their purpose is, we are too often afraid to face emotions, but not facing them makes them no less present. Instead, we risk being directed by them. Like a rat in a maze seeking the next piece of cheese, we tend to repeat things that cause us to feel pleasure and avoid the situations that cause us to feel displeasure, but emotions don't have an I.Q. and they're just one source of information. Emotions in a person with unprocessed trauma are often skewed by fear. Understanding emotions as information can help them not be so frightening. Free from fearing them, we are able to be more in touch with the information they are conveying, and choose the best course of action.

Connection

Connection is our fundamental reality. For those coming from a faith perspective, we see that as being connected to God and each other as brothers and sisters. Some come to the same truth through observing our relationship with the world around us. We see how interwoven our lives are with others. When we ignore our responsibility to each other, society quickly devolves into alienation, crime and violence. We can see how crucial our responsibility is to caring for each other, the earth and ourselves. We are interdependent on all creation for a healthy life together on this planet.

From the very moment of conception, connection is not merely ideological. It is actually biological. It is the connection of the egg and sperm that sparks life. Science has learned that a baby develops more healthily when connection is experienced. We are all familiar with the importance of things like a baby being held and receiving eye contact which communicates what the child is too young to understand in words. In *Social: Why Our Brains are Wired to Connect*, Matthew Lieberman, Ph.D. tells us that disconnection has been shown to be as physically damaging as a two pack a day smoking habit. His wonderful scholarly research shows connection is actually the foremost of all human needs, not food, clothing and shelter, like Abraham Maslow taught.

What is the essence of connection? Do you remember the Hasbro game *Connect Four*? There are four requirements for connection, just like it's necessary to line up four discs in order to win the game. Those four essential aspects for connection in relationships are: boundaries, vulnerability, being known, and being accepted. Boundaries give us a sense of emotional and physical safety. Basically, boundaries are respect for the fact that there is a place where I stop and you start, and I can't cross into your space without you freely and willingly inviting me into that area. When our boundaries are respected, we are afforded the freedom to be vulnerable. They give us the courage to expose who we really are.

This is crucial because it is only by sharing our authentic self that we have the chance to experience being known and accepted by another.

Most often this is a gradual process. Typically, we start by sharing our common ground, be it interests or experiences. That might be sharing the fact that we belong to the same club or workplace. We already have a reason to expect acceptance in return since the other person is like us in that way. If we don't know we have something in common, we usually start by sharing something good about ourselves like an accomplishment or an aspiration because it's less risky and, again, acceptance is almost certain. Eventually, we go about revealing our less glorious moments. Perhaps we do so by exposing an emotional or physical weakness or struggle. If we are still being accepted at that point, our courage is bolstered, and we may eventually risk something about which we are ashamed or feel deeply powerless. All through the process, being both known and accepted is crucial. Consider what the interplay is like between these factors in a relationship:

<u>Neither Known nor Accepted</u> - disconnection, only vaguely relevant to each other by virtue of being human beings. This can be particularly painful if it is someone with whom we have a desire for connection or from whom we have a right to expect safety. For example, if a parent or spouse doesn't take the time to know what is important to us, our interests, likes and dislikes and does not accept us.

Not Known, but Accepted - perhaps being accepted for belonging to the same political party or being fans of the same sports team. This gives us a generic sense of acceptance, but is completely impersonal and limited to a specific fact.

Known, but not Accepted - personal experience of rejection, emotional abandonment, betrayal, bullying or abuse.

Known and Accepted - personal connection and, if a deep level of vulnerability has been risked, even a sense of intimacy.

The critical factor in all of these is that of being known. It is being known which makes or breaks the experience being personal. The respect we are shown by the honoring of our boundaries gives us the courage to risk being known authentically. Acceptance of our authentic self gives us the experience of deep connection. Vulnerability without boundaries is victimization, and boundaries without vulnerability is isolation.

Ideally, connection happens for us as children from our parents or caregivers. It is needed to fuel human development in all areas. Safety and delight communicated through a peaceful, loving gaze between parent and child and later through support and encouragement helps the human body to develop. In a healthy body, the brain develops optimally, allowing the person to maximize their cognitive potential and be emotionally regulated. With such a foundation, there is an ability to understand and engage with others and the world from a fundamental sense of safety. That safety allows for compassion towards others and growth in healthy relationships.

Connection Opportunities

One day a friend and I were discussing the importance of connection. In the middle of our conversation, she had to run an errand. She needed to go to a store to return something, and I went along. As we stood in the customer service section, an older woman was at the counter dealing with her transaction and a middle-aged man stood off to the side with his arms folded. It seemed as though they were together along with a boy who appeared to be about seven or eight years old. The child was on the ground in front of a grocery cart studying the front panel of the cart. He observed how its hinges let it move inwards when another cart is pushed into it, thus allowing them to stack into a tight row. The whole time the boy was showing such curiosity and exploring, the gentleman stood watching him from a distance and saying nothing. Eventually, the older woman finished her transaction and it was my friend's turn to approach the counter. Finally, the man spoke to the child. As he pulled the cart away from the boy he said, "Get out of the way."

Later, I remarked to my friend about what we had witnessed and how remarkable it was that the gentleman, presumably the young boy's father, missed such an opportunity to connect to the boy. He easily could have commented on how he had discovered the hinges and how the cart is designed to fit together with the other carts. Instead of all the positive messages the boy could have been sent, the one message he was sent was that he was in the way.

As adults in the lives of young people in any capacity, we have such an amazing opportunity to hold up a mirror to them. By highlighting their strengths we do more than simply reflect, we create. Regardless of if we are biological parents, we have the opportunity to father or mother life into children by letting them know those good things we can see in them, if we look with the eyes of wisdom. To us, these things are so simple, but to a child, they are the dawning of self-knowledge.

As I was explaining this to my brother, I shared with him about having my nephew – his son - with me on Jekyll Island, one of the islands back home off the coast of southern Georgia. Bryce and I were climbing a small lookout tower and given that Bryce was three, he very much wanted to do so by himself, without me holding his hand. He was perfectly capable and so I followed along behind very closely and attentively, keeping him safe in case he slipped, yet showing confidence in his ability to do it on his own. As I followed closely behind and paid attention to how he held onto the rail and lifted his feet carefully onto each next step, I remarked, "Bryce, you are such a good climber." Having heard that, he began to take his steps very intentionally and deliberately. It was an instantaneous response.

When I told my brother, he exclaimed, "Oh! Is that where that came from?" Then, he shared that the following day he had been with Bryce at our parents' house. My brother was in a conversation with my father when, out of nowhere, Bryce had come up to them and very seriously told them, "You know, I'm a really good climber". I had shown Bryce his reflection in the mirror of my affirmation. He had immediately begun to act on this and then had internalized it into his belief about himself.

Bryce's Courage

One day I was with my brother, nephews and sister-in-law. We were visiting my sister-in-law's grandmother. My nephews, Bryce, still three-years-old, and his younger brother Moses, who was one and a half-years-old, were playing on the patio and their ball went over the fence. Suddenly, Bryce ran through the apartment to the front door, out of the apartment, and down the corridor. He raced past the patio where he'd just been playing. As he neared the neighbor's patio, we heard simultaneous feverish barking and fearful crying. With the same suddenness with which he had rushed outside, he returned to the apartment. I met him at the door and lifted him up, snuggling him to me, I said, "That must have been really scary. You didn't know those doggies were out there." Because he was scared, I didn't tell him there was no reason to be scared. Instead, I validated his emotion. I knew it would be important for him to feel a sense of connection quickly, since his frightening experience had been endured alone. I wanted him to know he wasn't isolated and was understood.

Wiping his tears with the back of his hand, he cried, "It was scary!" I told him I was going to hold him up high in my arms so he'd be safe, and we'd go back out and get his ball. I didn't know where the dogs were or if they were friendly, and I wasn't going to send him out alone to the same situation that had just scared him, but I didn't want to go get it for him and unwittingly confirm his thought that outside and dogs were something he couldn't handle. Holding him in my arms, we went back outside and followed the same route he'd just taken.

Of course, as we did, we heard the same frenzied barking from the dogs. As we got closer to the neighbor's patio, I could see the barking was coming from two little Yorkshire Terriers on the neighbor's patio, behind the rails. I saw Bryce's ball on the ground near the shrubs on the outside of the fence rails. I told Bryce, "Oh, look at the dogs. They are behind their fence." "Oh" said Bryce and he brightened with relief. I pointed out his ball laying in the shrubs and said, "I think those doggies are saying, "hey little boy, your ball is over here." "That's so nice!" said Bryce! He wriggled quickly down out of my arms and ran to get his ball. He had been able to assess the situation from a sense of safety since he felt known and accepted and was able to have his boundaries protected by me holding him. His confidence was quickly restored. He retrieved his ball and beamed with joy. Instead of feeling defeated, it was clear he felt victorious. He had been able to confront his fear and overcome it. He picked up a pinecone and hurled it as far as he could out into the lake and skipped back toward his great-grandmother's apartment.

At the end of their visit, his parents were getting his little brother into his seat and loading all their gear into the car. Bryce sat leaning against the back tire on the passenger's side as he waited. I went over to him and said, "Bryce, you showed so much courage by going back out there and getting your ball after the barking from those dogs had startled you." He put his hand to his chin and looked far off into the distance and said, "Yep, I have courage."

It had been important for Bryce to have the events interpreted for him so he could see the take-away lesson was that he was courageous and had conquered. The facts were all there, but he needed to have the experience of being known. As an adult in his life, I took advantage of an opportunity to hold the mirror for him and help him see himself clearly in light of what had transpired.

Children, like all of us, tend to behave according to who they believe they are. If they believe they are delightful to us, they behave delightfully. If they are made to believe they are bad kids, well, then that's often how they behave. Without the safety connection gives us, the sympathetic nervous system is sent into overdrive and the parasympathetic system doesn't kick in adequately to allow the body to calm and repair. From a place of stress, we live with cortisol, a stress hormone, pumping through our veins, which shuts down oxytocin, the hormone needed to feel love and trust. It's far too easy to not speak to or engage with a child until there is a behavior from them that we are irritated by or frightens us. We get tired, and it requires presence of mind to actually verbalize those little nuggets of beauty and potential we see. It's especially more challenging for those of us who are introverts, like I am, but the difference is that of taking the leadership role or giving it away; being able to set a positive tone with the child or left to mop up after they try to fill the emptiness inside them that longs to have an identity.

When we experience being known and accepted as a child, we have a bridge to being able to grow in self-knowledge and self-acceptance. Without that, we are left continually looking to those outside of us to know and accept us, yet unable to really internalize what they offer as true and valid, because their message conflicts with a message of rejection we got somewhere along the way leaving us fundamentally disconnected from ourselves.

Power

We all have power, though we might not always feel like we do. Because we are physical, emotional and spiritual beings, we have power in all three of these areas. Sadly, we don't always use our power to help, affirm, validate and support each other. Many times, because we aren't taught that emotions are information and what to do with them, we don't use our power for ourselves, either. That's not to say that power is bad, but it can be used for ill as much as it can be used for good. Simply, we can use our power for others and ourselves or we can use it over others and ourselves.

If someone is feeling anxious, she might want those feelings to stop. She might tell herself she's being stupid and to just get over it. If her child or a friend expresses concern or fear, the chances are she'll speak to them with the same voice. Even if a person was to manage to speak compassionately to another while being impatient toward herself, chances are there will be great expectations of gratitude or response from the other. We can only give more to others than we do to ourselves for so long without growing bitter.

61

There is a maxim the Latin of which is, 'Nemo dat quod non habet.' The translation is 'You can't give what you don't have'. This maxim applies to us in relationships. We can't give patience, understanding and acceptance to others when we don't have those very things for ourselves.

It's a much different scenario if a person's internal self-talk expresses understanding and compassion before gently guiding towards growth. If that is how we are relating to ourselves, imagine what a different stance we'll take with another person. We must use our power for ourselves before we use it for others. Sometimes that helps us to set healthy boundaries. At other times it allows us to have a true stance of compassion and empathy.

The vast majority of trauma clients have experienced being overpowered in awful ways. The conclusion may be drawn that power is bad, but that is not the case. Power's value lies in how it is used. Many people have fear of or difficulty with authority because they generalize from their experience. A traumatized person may be left with a pervasive feeling of powerlessness due to what they endured. They may feel resentful of power and have issues with authority that aren't personal. When I use my power for me in a way that doesn't seek to overpower you and you do the same, we have the climate needed for connection. When I use my power for me *and* for you *and* you do likewise, we have *connection*.

8

Success Stories

Sam and the Cycle of Growth

Sam came to me when he was 12-years-old, 50 pounds overweight, in a special classroom for kids with learning issues at his school from which he was regularly suspended for fighting, and on a laundry list of medications. He was so severely agitated I could almost see his eyeballs jiggling in their sockets. He couldn't read and couldn't pay attention in school long enough to learn. He was constantly set off by the least perceived incongruence or injustice, and had been in counseling and psychiatric treatment with diagnoses of Generalized Anxiety Disorder and Attention-Deficit/Hyperactivity Disorder since he was two-years-old.

Sam was adopted. His biological mother had been unaware she was pregnant. She was drug addicted and thought she was having appendicitis when she arrived at the hospital. It turned out she was pregnant and in labor. After giving birth to Sam, she left him in the hospital. He was a tiny little preemie and was going through withdrawals from crack cocaine. After five days he was adopted by a healthy and loving social worker. He and his behaviors had continued to grow bigger and more intense. By the time he was four-years-old, his adoptive mother feared he would end up in juvenile detention when he was older. Trying to work with him was certainly a challenge. He rocked the chair back and forth with such force the legs left the floor. He couldn't focus his gaze, and I continually had to redirect him to his work.

His mother was a delight to work with, as she realized the importance of keeping me abreast of the progress through treatment and after. For the next five weeks after treatment, she regularly updated me with remaining sticking points. What was particularly useful was that she also updated me on his improvements. It helped me to get a much fuller picture of all the changes and the parent/child dynamic. I was able to hone in on where he was still stuck and what traumas she had forgotten to report in his intake. Five weeks later I saw him again. The intensity behind his explosive eruptions at home had subsided. He was able to pay attention to the movie *42: the Jackie Robinson Story*. The significance was that it isn't an action movie. Previously, it had taken extreme chases, car crashes and shooting to hold his attention. Since treatment, he was showing the ability to attend to a human-interest story with a much slower pace than what he previously required. Also, while waiting at the dentist, his mother was impressed that he had picked up a magazine. Prior to treatment, he would never have had the interest or ability to do so. Attention had to be demanded from him.

In the weeks after treatment, his mother was able to set house rules, something she couldn't have done before because she was living in survival mode, constantly trying to avoid an explosion from Sam. He was able to obey the house rules, initially with a grumble and complaint, but it was a big improvement over the hour and a half tantrums he used to throw. He was able to come off all of his medications and lost 35 pounds. The next obstacle was getting his behaviors to be regulated in the classroom. His mother was in regular contact with his teachers and helped them to understand that he could be held to a higher standard. Once the school and the parent were on the same page, his behaviors at school came in line, as well. He learned to read, and they put him in all regular classes where he has remained to this day.

Today Sam is 17 and gets himself up early in the morning to go to work before he goes to school. I'm told he functions very well and mostly does well in school where he remains in all regular classes. He has goals, and his mother says she never has to worry about behavioral issues from him. He is bright, sensitive to others and funny. His cycle of growth is typical of what I've seen in the children I treated. Through being able to exercise his true ability, how he saw himself changed. As his self-concept improved, so did his behavior and relationships.

The purpose of treatment is to help clear up past programming, so the person is free, but what someone chooses to do with the greater degree of freedom is and will always be up to them. Going through treatment, I certainly was not made impervious to dumb choices. Living full-time from a place of calm compassion is a lifelong pursuit. Simply put, traumas are tantamount to shackles that keep a person chained to past emotions and perceptions. One person, when unchained may choose to get up and train for a marathon, while another may eat a bag of chips and take a nap or even pick up a hammer and clobber someone else.

Lizzie

As a young woman in her early 30s, Lizzie came to see me for treatment. From infancy she'd suffered from many symptoms. She had deficits leaving her with the cognitive capacity of an eight-year-old child. She had significant hearing loss in both ears from as far back as could be determined. She was also born with both of her hips displaced, but that had not been diagnosed right away. Consequently, as a baby she wouldn't nurse or take a bottle because the excruciating pain worsened when she was held to be fed and so would scream and cry. She was diagnosed with failure to thrive and fed through a feeding tube before her hip condition was discovered, then she was put in a body cast from under her arm pits to her ankles for the majority of her first year of life and off and on again until age seven.

She was brought to treatment with me because she regularly reacted to any negative emotion intensely and with the particular response of insisting on seeing a doctor or going to the emergency room. Because of her difficulty communicating, her mother felt obligated to take her to be seen by medical professionals, out of fear of missing legitimate symptoms. Lizzie also lacked any sort of flexibility with plans. For example, if in the morning her mother had said she was going to make spaghetti for dinner, but forgot to thaw out the meat and so ended up picking up a pizza instead, that change would result in a total meltdown of crying, disappointment and anger for 15 or 20 minutes. She always had a desperate need to know what was coming, which made it particularly difficult when plans changed, especially in regard to food. She even wanted to know what was for breakfast, lunch and dinner on the following day.

She wasn't able to self soothe and became highly agitated in difficult circumstances. She had attended her cousin's wrestling match and one of the participants was injured. Paramedics had to be called. The incident precipitated her crying, rocking and hitting herself in the head. Life had to be very consistent and predictable beyond what is humanly possible, in order for her to not be distressed. Every little event of the day, action or interaction made for a tenuous situation that could easily set her off, if it didn't go according to her expectations.

Because of her cognitive limits, her mother and aunt informed me of Lizzie's trauma history and her symptoms. I worked with her over the course of five days and did treatment much the way I would with an eight-year-old, since that was her cognitive level. She enjoyed treatment very much, since it is very interactive. She seemed to feel heard and understood and to finally know and accept herself. Besides that, she was taught about her 'wise self' who has the ability to stay calm and compassionate despite what was going on in her surroundings and circumstances. She latched onto that concept and still uses it all these years later.

In order to get the most out of therapy, some changes were required of Lizzie's mother, as well. During the week of treatment, one evening Lizzie had emerged from her bedroom and announced to her mother that her feet were cold. Her mother readily responded that she would be in momentarily to put her socks on, something

Lizzie was perfectly capable of doing for herself. Lizzie's mother needed to learn it was Lizzie's job to take care of such tasks, that way her daughter would feel safe and confident in her own abilities. Of course, her mother continued to be helpful and reassuring to 32-year-old Lizzie, but her mother did know Lizzie was able to do such things for herself when she slept over at her aunt's house. It was a paradigm shift, but she was able to realize that if Lizzie could do something somewhere else, she could do the same things at home. It was necessary for Lizzie's mother to be consistent in her expectations so Lizzie could grow in her ability to hit the mark.

After treatment, she stopped asking to go to the hospital and doctor. She was much more flexible with changes in plans and, when a change was difficult, was able to soothe herself by addressing her emotional 'Baby Lizzie' from her clear-thinking self, or 'Wise Lizzie.' She decided she wanted the independence of living in a group home and does so today. I'm told she is doing very well, has a job, and navigates her way to work and back home by bus.

Ben

It was the last day of a treatment week, and I'd had the pleasure of working with a very insightful and motivated gentleman named Ben. We had reached the end of the list of traumas, or so I thought. Then, Ben told me he believed he needed to process the trauma of an injury he had sustained to his arm almost a decade before. "There's just something about that memory," he said. More than what he said it was how he said it that struck me. He had a faraway look on his face. There seemed to be something he was feeling that he couldn't articulate. A feeling that had stuck with him from when he was injured made him realize we needed to address it in therapy. Ben told me the injury had caused nerve damage to his arm. That meant something different coming from Ben. You see, Ben was a medical doctor, so for him there was no gap between experience and diagnosis.

Through the course of the week of treatment, Ben's confidence in the treatment process had grown. On the first day of processing, everything was all new, but as we worked together through the week to reformat the painful events of the past and gain integration step by step, Ben and I had become the treatment team. Though some clients may believe themselves to be somehow fundamentally broken and therapists fundamentally 'better,' that's simply not true. The client isn't the problem. The traumas are the problem. The client *has* the symptoms they do because of what they've suffered. Their input is a great benefit and can give crucial clues.

As we processed Ben's trauma, his eyes widened. He looked at me as though I must know what he was experiencing. Of course, I didn't. My eyes widened, and I shook my head to tell him I didn't know what was happening. He told me the nerve damage he'd had for the last several years was gone. I heard from him again years after treatment, and the relief from the nerve damage remained.

Jimmy

70

I had told Ben's story on a conference call with a small group of leaders who had asked to meet with me. They wanted to learn how the people they serve might benefit from this method of treatment. It's one thing to hear that trauma has a biological effect on the brain - an organ most of us don't know much about and of which we ironically, think very little. It's quite another to discuss how freeing the brain up from a traumatic event can have physiological ramifications. Though I often tell the story of how my hair curled through the course of treatment and show my old student identification card with my treatment-induced curls, discussing the relief of chronic symptoms was something else altogether.

When I finished Ben's story, there was silence. I wondered what was happening on the other end of the line. After what seemed like a long silence, one of the leaders spoke up and told me he had a relative he wanted me to treat. Jimmy, who had been in a terrible car accident over a decade before, had sustained multiple severe injuries to his internal organs. At the time of our conversation, he was six feet, two inches tall and weighed only 102 lbs. He was being fed through a feeding tube, as he was only able to digest about four different foods and even those weren't guaranteed. Due to the tremendous weight loss, he had a difficult time sleeping and his energy level was greatly compromised, as one might expect, but other than the physiological symptoms and the difficulty that accompanied them, it didn't seem as though there were any mental health issues. I was used to asking about anxiety, depression, intrusive thoughts, flashbacks and nightmares. Jimmy, however, had none of these other than the natural anxiety and depression from

71

being a husband and father and having such a difficult time functioning. He even passed the site of the accident every day on his way to and from work and doing so wasn't bothersome to him in the least. He had sought help through Johns Hopkins, Cleveland Clinic and Mayo Clinic and had been told by all there was no biological reason for his symptoms.

What to do? He'd been told that his symptoms weren't physical, but they didn't sound emotional. Thankfully, my experience with Ben had taught me there could be biological manifestations of traumatic events that are very real. Once the motherboard, his brain, understood the event was over, the output to the rest of his body changed. Thus, I told Jimmy I thought there was a solid reason for us to work together. He told me he and his wife were so convinced there was no hope for him they were preparing to tell their young children he was dying. I encouraged him to wait to tell the children such news until after he had given treatment a try. There was no reason to traumatize the children if there was a possibility of help.

Since I was trying to treat something that wasn't emotional, and I had no way of being sure it was related to trauma, I asked him to be seen by my chiropractor, Dr. Robert Marrow. I had treated with him for over a decade and the long list of medical complications I had before treating with him and how much he helped me could itself fill a book. If I was going to treat something that may be in an area between my field and the medical field, I certainly wanted someone medically trained to have eyes on it, as well.

Jimmy readily agreed and made the trek down to the doctor on the first and last days of treatment. When Jimmy told me the finding was that three of his organs were stuck in the sympathetic response, I was excited. It meant I wasn't in left field. What I was seeing might very well have been a result of the trauma. We respond to trauma by attempting to fight or flee. That is a response from the sympathetic nervous system. When we go into the fight or flight response, our bodies prepare to mobilize. Blood is diverted to our arms and legs. Sending blood to move our arms and legs takes it away from our stomachs, which causes difficulty with digestion. Were you ever told not to swim until at least an hour after you've eaten? It's the same principle. With blood diverted away from the stomach and to the limbs, we aren't able to digest properly. Given that various other medical professionals had cleared him, it made sense to me that his inability to digest food was likely due to his brain still experiencing the car accident like it was still going on, even if his emotions did not seem altered.

Throughout the week, Jimmy's symptoms were still present, but that was to be expected because the trauma was not yet completely addressed until the last day. After we finished our session on Friday, he returned to Dr. Marrow to be reassessed. The findings were just what I had hoped. Being stuck in the sympathetic response was gone. Over the course of the days and weeks to come, his body began to be able to break down food. Chiropractic care supported his body with specific supplements needed to help his organs return to the parasympathetic/rebuilding mode. Once his brain registered the car accident as over, the rest of his body got the memo. I knew trauma was biological. Now, I realized that when treatment works with the brain, the results could be astounding, even on a biological level.

In Figure 4 we can see how the brain is left to limp along when we have unprocessed traumatic experiences. Unfortunately, a person can remain misdiagnosed for years or even a lifetime. All the while, they may pursue treatment for some perceived problem they don't have, while missing help for a legitimate condition they do have.

Jake

Jake's case was amazing, but given the neurology we've discussed so far, you'll see it makes perfect sense. Remember the left hemisphere of the brain is the side with the two verbal areas. Because of how trauma becomes encoded, the right hemisphere has a lot of pots boiling over on the back burners. It can be pictured as having buckets for sights, sounds, smells, tactile sensations and emotions. When it is over-active, the left hemisphere is, as a result, under-active, since we only have so much energy and attention to expend.

Jake was almost three-years-old. He had been through quite a number of injuries and accidents because he was a rough and tumble little fellow who was always going full speed and running and jumping. He had broken his arm, busted out a couple of teeth at another time, had tubes in his ears, and had witnessed a domestic violence episode between his parents.

Jake was very active in my office. He got to work very quickly, enthusiastically using puppets and playing with the camera. With children so young, the camera is set up to capture the play therapy we do, so the child can watch it back. Little Jake would stand in front of the camera and put his hands on his knees and sway slightly back and forth in front of the eye of the camera, until he could see himself in the little screen that was turned to face him. Once he caught a glimpse of himself, he would squeal with delight and point at his image.

What was particularly interesting about Jake was, though he was almost three, his speech was still quite limited. For example, if he wanted a drink of water, he would point at a water bottle and sort of grunt "Wah wah." He was seeing a speech therapist for treatment, and I really didn't give that limitation a second thought. I knew it was being addressed and made no ready connection from his speech deficit to my work. I soon learned I was wrong.

The week after our intensive work together, I returned to the office to find a number of messages from his speech therapist and his mother. I quickly called his mother, and she explained to me that in the two or three days following treatment Jake had skipped over stringing words together and started stringing sentences together. She asked me if such a change was normal. I simply had never worked with a child of that age with that speech limitation, but I told her a side-benefit like that made sense, given what we were doing. With the traumas finally experienced like they were in the past, the right hemisphere was able to calm and the left hemisphere, the one where the two verbal areas are located, was able to increase functioning, allowing, Jake's verbal ability to increase significantly. Treatment restores a balance between the two hemispheres of the brain, as you can see in Figure 5. Balance permits the two hemispheres to be able to work together in a coordinated way, which is what we need, regardless of the task. It would have been quite possible for his speech problem to persist despite the treatment if it was caused by something other than trauma. Trauma treatment is a logical first course of action in order to clear up emotions from a biological level. Unfortunately, many people leave NRI to a last ditch effort.

Figure 5 – Trauma Processing

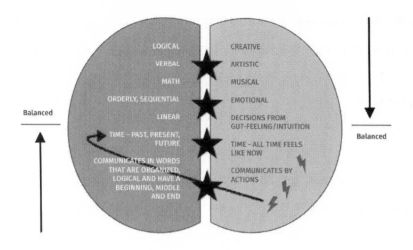

Balanced

Balanced

LOGICAL
VERBAL
MATH
ORDERLY, SEQUENTIAL
LINEAR
TIME - PAST, PRESENT, FUTURE
COMMUNICATES IN WORDS THAT ARE ORGANIZED, LOGICAL AND HAVE A BEGINNING, MIDDLE AND END

CREATIVE
ARTISTIC
MUSICAL
EMOTIONAL
DECISIONS FROM GUT-FEELING/INTUITION
TIME - ALL TIME FEELS LIKE NOW
COMMUNICATES BY ACTIONS

Jack

Preverbal traumas are significant, even as the person ages. Jack is another little child who was brought to me for trauma that had happened before he was old enough to speak. He was five-years-old when we met. He came from a lovely family, had siblings and an attentive and nurturing mother and father, but Jack had suffered a very serious burn when he was about 18-months-old. It was a complete accident. He had reached up onto the counter where a cup of scalding water sat and dumped it down on top of himself. He had to be treated for burns for a couple of weeks, which was a very painful process.   Some scarring that remained on one of his shoulders.

Prior to being burned, Jack's nickname had been Angel Baby because he had been such an easy and delightful child. After the burn, Jack's nickname became Demon Baby because when he didn't get his way, really regardless of the circumstances, he would screech and carry on. His parents learned of the work I do and they made the trip out to Ohio for us to work together.

His parents asked if he should come out for an entire week. They wanted to make sure I had plenty of time with him, but after doing a thorough assessment and taking a thorough history, it seemed there were no other traumas Jack had endured. If there had been more, I would have needed to treat those, too, since the way the brain encodes traumatic experiences often causes them to become somewhat entangled. For this reason, thorough treatment is essential. I assured his parents that I couldn't see us needing to work together more than a few hours.

In working with Jack, I used play therapy to reconstruct his experience. We used puppets to facilitate the integration work. He was very engaged in the play and the camera work. Taken together, with all of the particulars of this model, it allowed for the event to finally be experienced as an event in the past. His perceived need to respond to a situation with the intensity of life or death was able to be associated with that past event of the burn. The biological experience of dire threat was no longer omnipresent for Jack. He was, once again, a peaceful child.

I love working with little children because the majority of the time is spent crawling around on the floor and engaging them. I pay close attention to not just *what* they're doing, but *how* they're doing it. I find that when I'm able to help a child experience being known and accepted, there's a point when the fact that I'm a tall, middle-aged adult fades away. They look at me differently than they do initially. Their expression no longer says they know I'm a grown up, and they're a little kid, and there is a gap between us. There's an ineffable shift in their demeanor. The veil drops and suddenly we're just two people, not a big one and a small one, not an older and a very young one. We're just two souls. It's a beautiful experience and quite a privilege and honor.

Though he had previously been given to tantrums, Jack's parents had continued to be clear with him about what was acceptable and what was unacceptable. They'd done their best to be calm and compassionate, but still to hold to house rules for the sake of the sense of safety, security and predictability he and his siblings needed. It had, undoubtedly, been a difficult battle since he was stuck in the fight mode of that terrible traumatic day, but with treatment came the payoff. He knew what the expectations were, what the mark was he was trying to hit. When parents abandon being the leaders and setting the ideal, it is very difficult to motivate children to change because the child's negative behaviors are working for them. There is some way in which those behaviors are being rewarded.

This is one of the many reasons early intervention is key. Oftentimes parents of traumatized children live in survival mode. Out of sheer exhaustion they may find themselves on the path of least resistance in an effort to have some peace in their household. In other cases, caregivers may lose the ability to remain calm and compassionate toward the child because pain of rejection from the child may be painful reminders of past traumas of their own, perhaps ones that carried messages of rejection, abandonment or not being successful, effective or respected. The parent-child relationship can quickly devolve and leave both in pain, fostering a destructive pattern of relating. If the child is school age, the child's trauma-related behavior can make it very difficult to make friends and can lead to being labeled a bad kid. In many ways, early intervention is at once trauma treatment and trauma prevention.

Sophie

The tiniest client I ever worked with was a little girl of two-years-and-four-months. I'd never had a client that young and, I honestly wondered if she would be able to understand me enough to make therapy possible. Her parents wanted her to get some help and had the wisdom to seek it out as soon as possible. They didn't want her to conclude the symptoms were who she really was. Particularly with children, I love early treatment because so many complications are avoided. How sad for a hurting child to be seen as a bad child! I was willing to give it a try and see if therapy was possible with her even though she was so young.

She had been through quite a number of medical traumas since her birth. Through a variety of circumstances and symptoms, little Sophie had not been able to get enough food and had actually been diagnosed with failure to thrive in her first month of life. As a result, she behaved the way I'd expect from someone who had been starved. She became very intense around food and very possessive of it. She'd always demand more, but she couldn't be given very much at once because of some of her medical condition. Her food was portioned out in such a way so that she had plenty of time to digest it without getting sick. When she would be given three crackers as a snack, she'd demand the whole box, when that wasn't given to her, she'd fitfully crush the crackers she *was* given. Then she would realize what she had done and would crawl around on the floor scrounging for every morsel she could find and eating each one as though it was her last. To see her behave so would leave no one doubting she was continuing to experience the trauma of starving as though it was still happening. Because she would virtually inhale her bottle down to the last dregs, she couldn't be given more than a few ounces of liquid at a time, or she'd make herself sick on that, as well.

I happily agreed to try to work with her. Preverbal clients are wonderful, and they come along rather seldom. I love the challenge of communication with this population and the thrill of being able to help them feel like they and their plight was known. To me, it's one step short of being Snow White, able to communicate with the little woodland creatures. When I worked with her, I used puppets instead of drawing, and I communicated her story for her since she wasn't developmentally able to do so yet. We weren't long into the session, and it was obvious she understood what I was communicating to her. Each poignant aspect of her traumas I communicated to her, she repeated back to me in her limited words, but with limitless emotion. After processing the trauma, it was necessary to help the part of Sophie that knew she was no longer starving to be the one taking the lead. Prior to treatment the part of her that had spent her whole little life feeling like she was starving was running the show.

I used a baby doll for the integration component of the processing. It was one of the dolls with a bottle with disappearing

81

milk. After I modeled for her how to take care of the doll as a symbol of the emotional part of her own heart, I gave it to her to embrace and soothe. When she gave the doll the bottle, she immediately asked for her own bottle. I knew I couldn't avoid that forever. She had to eat and so needed to learn how to relate to food differently. I handed her the bottle and she began to drink it intensely. As she did, I gave the doll the bottle and then said that Baby Sophie was going to take a break. Very focused on me, little Sophie began to whimper intently, but removed the nipple from her mouth and sat the bottle on the floor. She understood the doll was representative of her and me moving the bottle away from the baby doll indicated for Sophie to remove the bottle from her own mouth. Then, before she had a chance to take it back, I announced that Baby Sophie was going to have some more. I wanted her to not just see me as someone who was taking food away, but was giving it, as well. She seemed taken aback by that. She focused on me and raised the bottle back up to her mouth and, after a few seconds, I announced again that Baby Sophie was going to take a break. We went back and forth like that three or four times. Each time she followed my lead and her sucking became much more relaxed until it became so commonplace to her that she actually left her bottle and went to play with a toy in another part of the room.

I brought her parents in to update them and, when her mother saw Sophie playing in one corner with a toy and her half-full bottle in another, she pointed fingers at each and stated, "THAT has never happened in her life."

I encouraged her parents to make the times Sophie had to wait for food special times, so her mother set up a special place for her to color when it wasn't time to eat. Sophie was no longer possessive of food. She had not grown for quite some time, and within six weeks after treatment I was told she had grown half an inch. I was amazed by this bright little girl and grateful additional problems were prevented.

Michael

Michael was 20 when he came to me at the referral of one of his family members. I wasn't sure if I was going to be able to be of any assistance to him since his only profoundly significant trauma was that his mother had been in labor with him for 24 hours when giving birth to him.

The list of symptoms he had endured throughout his life was extensive. Upon coming to me he was colorblind, had a very dull sense of smell and consequently a very dull sense of taste. His tactile sense was extremely blunted. He reported that he felt like he had gloves on when touching something, as he could feel, but not acutely. His hair was very coarse, and his scalp was dry and flaky. He had frequent migraines, and one had lasted for two months causing him to be hospitalized.

Throughout his life, he had always been rather easily overwhelmed by a lot of sound and activity, regardless of how positive it might have been. For example, even as a child at his own birthday party, he would typically have to relegate himself to his room because he was on sensory overload. Academically, he had always struggled in a couple of specific ways. Though clearly an intelligent young man with an extensive vocabulary, he'd never been able to sound out words, and he had also struggled with math. Both of these are functions particular to the left hemisphere of the brain and both are areas of struggle for many of the traumatized people I've treated over the years.

When he came to my office on the first day, he was very slight of build and by size and color looked rather sickly and weak. Throughout the week we processed the few traumas he had experienced, even though the primary one, the one about his birth, he was not able to recall. I knew it was still remembered by his brain so we got to work.

Through the course of the week of NRI he reported being able to see color and sense through touch, taste and smell much more than ever before. Also, he appeared to have much more vitality than he did at the beginning of the week. Upon his return back to his home state the next day, his mother informed me that he was walking around her office and reading the titles of books on her bookshelves and, for the first time, able to sound out words. Within a couple of weeks his hair became soft and shiny, and his scalp was no longer dry. He began to put on much needed weight and do math for fun. Six months later I was informed that he had grown three inches since the time of treatment. His color was no longer pale. He looked happy and healthy.

Because of the many symptoms he'd had, he had grown up seeing himself as someone who wasn't capable. As his changes began to become his new normal, he began to see himself differently and tried things he hadn't tried before. He was able to stay at home by himself over the weekend while his family went away. He began to try his hand at cooking. Eventually, he got his driver's license and is planning to attend college this coming fall. I've found that once the brakes are put on the vicious cycle of symptoms and self-perception, the cycle can then do a 180-degree turn and be a positive cycle of growth. The person may experience, possibly for the first time, that they are capable. If they reach out to try new experiences, that sense of capability can continue to build on itself.

There is no way to know beforehand what symptoms are due to trauma, but since trauma effects how we perceive ourselves, others and the world, it certainly can effect a wide variety of areas including emotional, behavioral, cognitive, spiritual and work/school performance. Also, continued physical stress can cause a high degree of wear and tear on the body, as proven by Vincent Felitti, M.D. in the Adverse Childhood Experiences study (ACEs). Just like the wide range of symptoms from trauma, there is a wide range of benefits of treatment.

9

Decoding Dynamics

I was doing my internship on a secure adult unit of a hospital. One particular week the unit was very crowded, and all the patients were struggling greatly. Tensions were high, to say the least. On a particular day, a young adult was admitted onto the unit. My supervisor greeted him and explained to the young man, Greg, that we were going into group and asked him if he wanted to join us. He said he did, that he'd been struggling with suicide and he wanted to share with the group. My supervisor readily accommodated him and told him he'd give him the floor.

That plan seemed pretty straightforward until it wasn't. Before Greg could get a word out, an older woman, Stacey, who was sitting across from me, barked out, "Ah, he should have just killed himself. He's probably going to end up killing himself anyway." Everyone looked incredulous. Eyebrows raised and jaws dropped. No one knew Greg. He was brand new to the unit. Stacey certainly didn't have an issue with him. How could she say something like this to someone she didn't even know? It seemed beyond cruel. My supervisor, a very wise and experienced therapist, remained very calm and turned to Stacey and said that he knew she'd been through a lot of difficulties in her life. "It's not about what I've been through! He's going to kill himself. Why doesn't he just get it over with?" Now, my supervisor was like the Red Barron in a dogfight and was trying to get an angle on Stacey. "What makes your pain so much greater than someone else's pain?" he asked. Her response remained unchanged for the next 15 minutes as he continually tried to reel in Stacey's behavior. Despite the fact that everything he was saying was good, right, true and therapeutic, her response was the same.

I began to panic, but was trying to maintain a poker face. I was watching the clock, well aware that group only lasted an hour. Once we went back to our offices, what would happen? The group was growing very intense and very irate with Stacey and understandably so. I felt like I was on a plane plummeting quickly to the ground below. May Day! May Day! 20 minutes had gone by and I realized I hadn't contributed to group at all. I had no idea how to help. Group only lasted an hour and we were now a third of the way through. Stacey wasn't backing down, there was no light at the end of the tunnel, and the patients were highly agitated. Once group was over, I could only imagine how all the other patients would want to draw and quarter her. I thought the one thing I could do was pray silently.

As I did, I felt like the Lord was leading me to look at Stacey's eyes, which is the last thing I wanted to do because she was mean and scary. I feared I'd see unbridled cruelty, if I did. Mustering up my courage and bracing myself, I looked into her eyes. What I saw was shocking. I saw terror. Stacey was terrified. I was in utter disbelief. Before I had time to think of what to say, I was so moved I found myself already speaking. Very gently I was saying, "Stacey, you're safe. You're safe." She put her head down on the table, and her whole body began to quake. She looked like a volcano getting ready to blow. None of us could have predicted that she would have gone off like a loose cannon and we certainly didn't know what to expect next. I wasn't sure if she had heard me because the tension was so high.

All of a sudden, with her head still on the table, she started wailing and crying out, "*Am* I safe? *Am* I safe? I don't *feel* safe!" My supervisor looked down the table at me as if to ask why I had known to say that. I gave him a look back to communicate I couldn't explain at that point. He suggested to Stacey that she go with me, and I could help her feel safe. She did leave with me, and I managed to get her settled. He apparently helped the other group members come to a place of understanding and compassion for Stacey because there were no problems after group therapy that day, no fights, no remaining angst or turmoil.

That event was a real lesson to me of how fundamental it is to have a sense of safety. Over the years, I've seen the same type of scenario play out. As I said before, if someone is not in their right mind, they're probably in their right brain, the emotional side, not the logical, reasonable left side we use for problem solving.

Another event I only understood in retrospect as I decoded the dynamics was a time I was working at an inner-city school in Akron, Ohio. I provided trauma treatment for many of the children and also, at times, was called into classrooms to de-escalate situations. One particular morning, the call came over the intercom, "Miss Vasquez to the fourth-grade classroom." That was all the information I had. Since classes were in session, I assumed there was a problem. I wondered if there was an active shooter or if someone needed to talk. There was really no telling.

When I arrived at the classroom, what I found was a math teacher trying to teach and 29 students trying to learn. The 30th student was standing in the middle of the classroom with her arms folded and her bottom lip stuck out. She was the picture of defiance and, though only in fourth grade, she was about as big as I am. I had never worked with this girl or had any real interaction with her other than the fact that she'd often wave to me in the hallways. I had no real relationship with her to draw on or give me any cues as to what might be going on or how to handle the situation. In the seconds I had to assess the situation, I could tell the teacher wanted the student to sit down or go to the office and she was refusing to do either. I was supposed to make that happen without knowing the girl, not even her name, and we weren't allowed to put our hands on the students. I had no magic wand. My mind was blank.

Mentally, I searched for insight, understanding or a way to intervene. All I could come to was that she was a person with dignity, and I had to treat her that way. I drew in a bit closer to her, so the whole class wouldn't hear what I said to her. I wanted to protect her privacy. I was careful, though, not to invade her space because I didn't know her past and didn't want her to feel threatened. Softly I said, "I'm sorry, I know I don't know you and you don't know me, and I honestly don't know what's going on here. I do know you're a good kid. I've seen you in the stairwells a number of times and you always smile and wave at me." When I said that, her look of defiance instantly shifted and tears rushed down her cheeks. I was taken aback.

I certainly hadn't meant to make her cry. I was simply trying to speak to her honestly and respectfully. I didn't have an angle or an expectation. I was just trying to find a peaceful place to start a conversation. I asked if she wanted to leave the room with me so we could talk and now, crying in front of all her peers, she eagerly agreed. It turned out there was a situation for which she needed to go to the office. I don't remember what the situation was, but I remember being very grateful things ended so smoothly. We could have very easily ended up on social media with some horrendous scene of an intervention gone wrong.

I didn't understand how those two situations, the one with Stacey and the one in the classroom, had played out so well. I only really came to understand them many years later when I worked with a 10-year-old boy named Dakota. As I showed him Figure 6, he asked me why his parents didn't always seem calm and compassionate and his teachers didn't either. I struggled for a way to explain the dynamics he was experiencing in a way he could understand. As I ran errands that evening I continued to search for a way, and it hit me. The next day when I worked with him, I folded two little squares of paper into triangles and showed them to him. I explained that each represented a person and we all have the ability to be calm and compassionate, controlling and to freak out. He understood. I explained the dynamic in Figure 7. I told him when we relate with compassion for each other, everything feels good and right, and we feel heard and respected. That's when things go well and we feel a sense of connection.

Figure 6 - Integration

Figure 7 – True Self to True Self

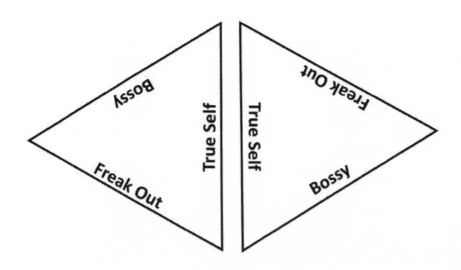

Next, I turned the triangles as you see in Figure 8 and told him that if one of the people starts trying to control the other, the second person might freak out or, as in Figure 9, might try to be even more controlling than the first person. Either way, that's when things don't feel good and problems happen. The challenge is, those bossy and freak-out modes tend to attract each other, and we can easily get locked up in those ways of relating and not be able to find a way out.

Figure 8 - Freak out to Bossy

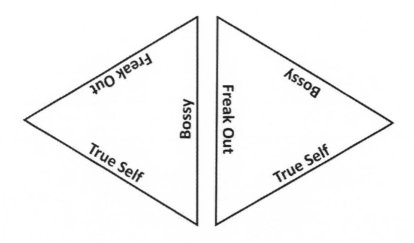

Figure 9 – Bossy to Bossy

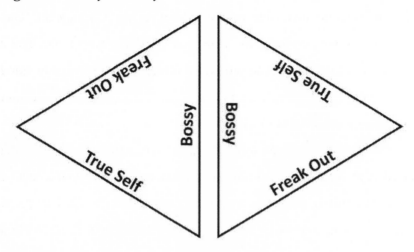

What I devised to explain dynamics to Dakota helped me to understand the response from Stacey in the hospital and the child in the classroom. Through this model, I was able to reverse engineer those two examples that had mysteriously turned out so well. Understanding dynamics provided me with insight into future relating. I'm very grateful for Dakota's question and that he didn't take my initial, incomplete explanation at face value.

Let me be clear. I have a lot of success stories, but I don't always get it right. Here's a way I completely blew it. It was the winter of 2013 and the dark and cold seemed interminable. I'm from South Georgia and don't really have any use for weather under 80 degrees and certainly don't tolerate the gray Ohio skies with much delight. When the spring finally came, I was overjoyed. My soul felt like a crocus beginning to bloom. This particular day, the sky was a vivid blue, and the snow had melted. Though the air was still crisp, it was quite tolerable. My arm was sprained, but I was desperate to be outside, so I headed to the park with my dog, Sugar. The love of my life, and smarter than her owner, she's a big Chesapeake Bay Retriever mix who adopted me when she was nine weeks old. She's so sweet that no other name would be appropriate. A reliably good listener and well behaved on a leash, I didn't expect it to be difficult to walk her, even with my injured arm.

When we began to walk down the path, she was jerking and twisting the leash like nothing I'd ever experienced with her. I popped the pinch collar a couple of times and called her name sternly, but with her nose turned on to all the smells that had been trapped for months under the snow, her ears were definitely turned off. She was not paying a bit of attention to me and with each jerk of the leash a jolt of pain went through my arm. I couldn't tolerate it, and after only about five minutes of an attempt at a walk, I was marching her furry behind back up to my car. Inside the vehicle and driving home, I was looking at her in the rear view mirror and fussing at her as though she was a child. "What was that??? That was TOTALLY RIDICULOUS and you know better than that!!!" I was having a fight with my dog. A little voice in my head told me so and told me anyone driving past could see I looked like an idiot.

Back at my apartment, I put her out on the deck. I needed to try to regain sanity. I feverishly began to clean the kitchen to burn off some steam. The little voice continued, "Let it go! It's over. She's a dog!" but it didn't matter. I couldn't get a grip on my emotions. I felt crazy. I couldn't calm myself. Finally, a little thought went through my mind, "That was really disappointing". Oh my goodness! I was doing it to myself. I was trying to control myself out of freaking out, and it certainly wasn't working with me any better than it would have worked in a relationship. Realizing I was relating internally from Bossy Mode to Freak Out Mode, I quickly changed and instead validated my own feelings. My self-talk changed to, "Of course that was disappointing. You just wanted to be able to enjoy the outdoors. It's been a really long and brutal winter." Peace returned. It seems all the part of me that was ranting and raving really wanted was to be heard. Switching from trying to control my emotions to validating them compassionately, I quickly calmed and readily felt compassion for Sugar. She must have had cabin fever as much as I did. Her great excitement had led her to being particularly energetic and unable to contain herself. I couldn't have compassion for her until I had it for myself.

"Poor Little Bobby"

Bobby was 10-years-old and had been adopted. The lack of attention and connection he had in the orphanage, was terrible. When his adoptive mother prepared to fly to Ohio with him for treatment, she asked me what reason she should give him for why they were getting on a plane to travel so far. It was obvious to me. Tell him the truth; tell him he's coming to make stories about the times he had to be brave.

Since his behaviors were very regressed, oppositional and defiant, he often threw tantrums. His school and his peers had labeled him as a bad kid. His experiences in therapy had focused on

96

his lack of attachment to his adoptive parents and his negative behaviors. Having been in trouble often in the classroom, he had been to the principal's office regularly. I had treated so many people with traumatic experiences of authority that I chose not to have a desk in my office. Instead, it was set up like a living room. I didn't want to position myself in any way over a client. A desk would be a constant non-verbal reminder I was the one with power. Many traumas are, essentially, an abuse of power. When clients and I met, we were two people in a room. We both needed to be reminded of that fact, not my power.

Work with Bobby went well. With each day, his regressed behaviors were diminishing. Whereas he had behaved much like a three or four-year-old at the start, he was, by mid-week, remarkably more age appropriate. I was really having great hope for his prognosis. When his mother picked him up from his session, we stood in the doorway exchanging pleasantries for a moment, then something completely dizzying began. As his mother and I were talking, Bobby who was initially hanging on his mom's neck began humping her leg. It was literally as though time slowed down and the room started wobbling. I couldn't believe my eyes. I did a double and then a triple take, but there he was, and there was no doubt about what he was doing. All the while, his mother continued to talk to me like nothing was happening.

I asked him to take a seat in the waiting room and give me a chance to talk to his mother for a minute, which he readily did. I searched the farthest recesses of my brain, but for the life of me could not remember ever having been trained for how to handle such a situation. "How could I gently broach the subject? Certainly, she must not be aware of what he was actually doing," I thought. I have no doubt I must have been spitting and sputtering like an old car on its last leg. Somehow, I managed to get the words out. I asked her if she realized Bobby had been humping her leg like a dog, fully expecting her to be shocked and appalled at the suggestion, but categorically unaware. Instead, she nonchalantly replied that he often did so. I was more shocked and concerned by her response than Bobby's behavior. Not only was she fully aware and permitted it, but it hadn't been concerning enough for her to mention it or shameful enough for her to try to hide it.

I told her it wasn't acceptable behavior. She told me poor little Bobby had been through such terrible things in his past and if this was what made him feel good, she wasn't going to deny him. I explained there wasn't anything I could do in therapy to help him, if she was complicit with such behavior.

NRI allowed him to choose to behave consistent with his true age rather than in a much younger manner. I had already experienced the shift in how he interacted with me alone. With his mother relating to the regressed part of him, there was going to be very little hope of him wanting to relate out of his true/wise self. We tend to relate out of whichever part someone relates to. She wasn't using her power to protect a healthy boundary and thereby teach him about healthy boundaries. He wasn't required to use his power for himself. He was being taught by her enabling and permissiveness, to ignore his power for himself and exercise power over her. A mother's relationship to her child is one of the most powerful. It would be virtually impossible for him to take the lead. She needed to lead with appropriate behavior for him to be able to respond appropriately.

Not only did leg humping have all kinds of things wrong with it on so many levels, but society certainly wouldn't and shouldn't be so accommodating of his desires. Additionally, she was sending him a double message. She was looking to relate to poor little baby Bobby at one moment but was opposed at the next moment when he would throw a tantrum. We were at an impasse, and she refused to comply with my recommendations. I never heard how he did after treatment, but I can't imagine very much integration happened.

The point of this story is that healthy connection to a caregiver or parent is crucial. Trauma processing cleans the slate to begin to form healthy connection, but connection is a two-way street. If I plug in my television and it doesn't work, the reason might be that there isn't power going to the outlet or it could be that the television is broken. The most treatment will ever do is provide a person the ability to connect. It will never remove a child's need to be known and accepted where they are allowed boundaries and the caregiver has healthy boundaries.

Though this is an extreme example, the same dynamic happens quite often. Many times, I've witnessed parents relate to children in ways that unwittingly send the message that the world and reality are too difficult for the child to handle. It can make the parent feel very good, but it does nothing to prepare the child for living in this world. The dynamic can be reversed as well by the parent looking to be tended to by the child. This happens when the parent looks for validation and affirmation from the child such as when a parent came to pick up a child from a treatment session. Having enjoyed his therapy session, the child was reluctant to leave. His mother began looking for emotional affirmation from the little client, "Don't you love me? Didn't you miss me?" The healthy dynamic for relating is for each individual to take care of his own emotions in accordance with his ability and then to relate out of a place of calm compassion toward others.

Justin, Bridget & Gabe

I had the pleasure of working with biological siblings who had been adopted together, Justin who was 11 and Bridget who was nine. They came from many states away accompanied by their mother who, upon adopting the children, determined she would stop working and devote herself full-time to their care. Even after having been in treatment for two years and on a regimen of medications, the children were very troubled.

They had suffered tremendous neglect, physical abuse, and had been exposed to domestic violence in their original home. After being removed and placed in foster care, horrendous atrocities had been perpetrated on them by their foster parents. They had been kept in confinement with their hands and feet bound, and at times, subjected to sexual abuse by the foster parents. They had also been forced to act out sexually with each other. It was really more abuse than I could wrap my head around. As a result, they were having a very difficult time connecting to their new caregivers. No wonder!

When their only intimate exposure to adults had been one of abuse and neglect, why would they want anything to do with anyone, especially adults? Bridget's behaviors, at times, were so confounding and intense that her father, a very practical man, even said he had wondered if she was possessed.

I worked with both children separately to process their traumas and a bit together to foster a healthy dynamic between them. Though the content of their experiences was so difficult, the relief they experienced and the fact that the process has many different active components, kept them engaged throughout the week.

Their parents worked with them after treatment to set clear boundaries and expectations and, most especially, to help them feel known and accepted. Justin's cortisol levels had been tested prior to treatment and had measured at the level of stress a firefighter has on the way to a fire. After treatment, he was tested again and his levels were normal. The children had no further need of psychotropic medications or ongoing counseling. We found, as they matured, their traumas were available to be addressed on deeper levels and doing so helped them to integrate their pasts into their maturing self-concepts.

A few years later, things were so peaceful with them that their parents wanted to expand their family again by adopting another child. They had been praying and considering if bringing another child into the family would upset the apple cart with Justin and Bridget, not knowing if their emotions and security were too fragile. Within two weeks of discussing it as a couple, the brother and sister approached their adoptive parents, asking if they could adopt again because they wanted to help another child the way they'd been helped. They did just that and adopted Gabe. He had been through NRI, too, so his integration into the family was relatively peaceful. He is a wonderful addition to their family.

The neurological reformatting of the traumas allowed Justin, Bridget and eventually Gabe to finally feel safe enough to be open to relationships with each other and their adoptive parents and it was Justin and Bridget's integration work that allowed them to be compassionate to another child joining their family. Their parents' knowing and accepting them was what established them in a sense of emotional safety and simultaneously modeled for them how to relate to themselves with compassion. They connected to others, like Gabe, the way they related to themselves.

Joshua and School

When Joshua came to me, he was 15-years-old and had been adopted before the age of two. He had been removed from his birth parents' custody due to extreme neglect. The parents by whom he was adopted were in their mid-50s at the time of the adoption. At the point when I treated Joshua, they were in their early 70s.

Joshua had greasy hair, yellow teeth and horrible breath. He had an odor about him that comes from chronically poor hygiene and was pale and lacking muscle tone. It wasn't that Joshua didn't have what he needed to be healthy. He wore an expensive basketball jersey and very expensive basketball shoes. Honestly, he was a mystery to me. How could he have gone from rags to riches, now have every opportunity, and yet not be choosing to embrace life?

Joshua's behavior was baffling. Though he was obviously bright, he was not attending school. He stayed up until the wee hours of the morning watching senseless videos and surfing the Internet and then refused to get out of bed until the afternoon. His parents had hired a tutor to work with him each evening. They were, understandably, tired and frustrated with his opposition and tried to motivate him with material rewards, but it didn't work. He did what he wanted and, only what *he* wanted to do. They didn't know how to reach him. Their rewards became expensive bribes, and the stakes got higher with less and less payoff until his behavior had devolved into terrible hygiene and an overall disengagement from life, school, and peers. He substituted self-worth with highly valued material goods and real participation in life for virtual participation.

I asked Joshua what he wanted to be when he grew up, pointing out to him that his parents were very supportive, and he was very bright. I hoped to help him have a vision for his future. He told me matter-of-factly that he wanted to be an alcoholic when he grew up. He explained rather frankly that his parents were older and had plenty of money and by the time he would need to work, he would have their inheritance and not need to do so. He would be able to watch movies, play video games, and drink all day. I was shocked at the lack of motivation and the apparent thought and choice he was putting behind his approach to his future. I wondered what good trauma treatment could do for him. If he was choosing this behavior, what chance did anyone stand to make a difference?

103

I knew trauma is often the root of emotional, behavioral, relational, cognitive, physical and spiritual difficulties. Once the root is addressed, many and varied problems, even ones that seemed unrelated, are often resolved. I focused on addressing with Joshua the extreme neglect he had suffered as a baby. The effects of that neglect, though he wasn't consciously aware, remained present in his visceral experience of himself and the world. It's no leap to imagine him living disengaged from the world as a result of how he had to disengage as a baby to tolerate his emotional pain.

Some weeks later, Joshua's mother contacted me and told me he was doing quite well. He had been attending school! The same boy who refused and could not be made to go to school was now voluntarily doing so. I was shocked - quite delighted - but truly shocked. It was a lesson to me that though a behavior may seem volitional, the degree of freedom in that choice can be dramatically limited by trauma symptoms. Two years later, I received a further update. Joshua made honor roll. He went from having aspirations of becoming an alcoholic who would play video games and watch videos all day to a young man who was truly applying himself and engaging in life.

A common diagnosis given to many foster and adopted children is Attachment Disorder. The difficulty connecting to caregivers is to trauma as a cough is to a cold. It is a symptom. When the trauma is treated, as when the cold is treated, the symptom is relieved. I once treated a child who had been adopted at two-years-old and was 14 at the time of treatment. At the end of the week, her mother shared with me that she had told her daughter she

104

felt more connected to her through the week of treatment than she had over the past 12 years. The girl's answer was succinct, but profound. She said, "Mom, it's so much easier to connect to you now that I feel connected to me." It always fascinates me that the same experiences we can intuitively understand in adults somehow baffle us in children. For example, if an adult goes through an intensely painful relationship, is betrayed, feels rejected and abandoned and then doesn't want to date, we readily understand, even if they've had positive relationships in the past. If a child goes through a like experience with their very first and only intimate relationship ever, then we see it as something wrong with the child. As a former child, I take issue with that. Instead, I see that behavior as smart. It means the child learned and a child capable of learning holds great promise.

For moving forward in freedom and the ability to thrive, the client and/or caregivers are provided with an understanding of how to navigate true connection with others. When it comes to working with children, this means the parent is a crucial part of that equation. The 'fix my kid' approach to treatment is not useful and will not produce the results the often-frustrated caregiver desires. If you are a parent of a child going through treatment, your ability to engage in a calm and compassionate way with no ulterior motive is going to be necessary for the greatest gains of treatment. Your power is far greater than you can imagine in the life of your child. An approach of dropping a child off, but not engaging with the process or following through on treatment recommendations will not produce healthy results. Parental engagement is crucial because your powerful position in the life of the child is vitally important.

We all hold great power in the lives of each other and especially the lives of young people. This is greatly accentuated for caregivers. Early treatment is imperative lest caregivers endure the difficult behaviors so long they no longer like the child. Chances are, if a child is irritating and bewildering, they are just as frustrating and confusing to themselves. If your hurt is already to that point, be emotionally honest with yourself and get the help you need first, so you can connect to your child through the benefits of NRI.

While on another visit with my brother and his family, it was late one evening, and I was back in the guest room getting ready for bed. I heard crying coming from the living room that I concluded must be one of my nephews. The crying went on and on. I went out into the living room to see if it was anything seriously wrong. I was amazed at the stillness and quiet in the room as my sister-in-law held my little nephew, Moses, serenely on the couch, reading him a bedtime story and my brother surfed the Internet on his laptop. It was a stark contrast to three-year-old Bryce wailing in the middle of the room. I asked what happened and they said he had stubbed his toe. They had already acknowledged his injury and attempted to console him to no avail. I returned to the back of the house and continued to get ready for bed, but the sobs didn't stop.

Once I had finished, about five minutes later, I returned to the living room. Bryce's mom had been attentive and fulfilled his request for a superhero Band-Aid, even though there was no bleeding or even redness. I continued to marvel at how Bryce continued to cry and remained inconsolable for so long when there didn't seem to be any real injury. This kind of behavior from him was such a regular occurrence that no one in the family seemed the least bit surprised by it. I sat on the chair by the couch where Bryce was tucked, still crying, in the crook of my brother's arm. After a couple of minutes, I gently told Bryce he has a Baby Brycey in his heart who was scared, and he could let him know he was safe. He looked at me with a combination of annoyance and confusion and pulled in closer to my brother saying, "Daddy." When my brother heard what I'd told Bryce, he quickly pulled up baby images on the computer. He selected a picture of a baby and opened it. He turned the laptop toward my nephew. I was truly amazed at what happened next. Bryce was still huffy and upset and making little cries, but upon fixing his gaze on the image of the baby, he became focused. Then I watched all the tension drain out of his body as his face became peaceful. That was the end of the crying.

You see, when Bryce was being born, the umbilical cord had become wrapped around his neck and there was the need to do an emergency C-section because his heart rate kept dropping. It was a very frightening and powerless feeling for him, I would imagine. I also suppose that a baby would feel very isolated and frustrated in the midst of all that. He naturally would have wanted to come out, but he couldn't and instead would have felt sick or distressed as his heart rate dropped. He was traumatized by the experience. Thankfully, he was delivered safe and sound and is a very bright and handsome boy. No one would suppose there was any sort of injury. That experience had probably become encoded in his brain in a way

107

that colored his world. Thus, when he stubbed his toe, there was a kaleidoscope of sensations and emotions that put him back in an experience of isolation and frustration that prevented him from being able to receive the connection his parents offered him. The traumatized part of his heart needed connection, but he was the one who had to do it. Connection to himself had been disrupted by his birth experience. Part of him had continued to experience that event, but the real Bryce had moved on and knew he was safe. He had to go into his heart and reassure himself he was safe.

David's Freedom from Shame

As a young adult, David was brought to me. He came from quite some distance and was accompanied by some of his extended family. Since I had received his trauma history prior to him scheduling, I concluded the case would be a typical one. He had certainly been through some difficult experiences in his past. I set in to work with him on Monday morning when he arrived.

When I did his intake, though, his responses were rather curious, and I quickly found myself wondering what was really going on. In asking about his employment, he told me he was working as a clerk in a video store. Since he didn't have any notable physical or mental disability, I wondered why this 21-year-old strapping young man wasn't dating, in college or pursuing a career or a trade. I asked him how he liked the work and he told me, "It can be difficult to work with the public." "Of course," I readily agreed. I know from my own experience that food service, retail, and other types of customer service can be quite trying.

He told me he tried to handle it by remaining silent. "You know, like George Washington," he added. I thought that was a curious comment, as I don't know Washington to be reputedly a man of few words, but I proceeded with the intake and asked him what he saw himself doing in five or 10 years. He told me, "I really want to be a superhero who is funny." At that, I thought he surely must be joking and looked up from my notes to catch his eye and give him a smile and a chuckle, but by his expression I could tell he was completely serious. I'd like to be a funny superhero too, but I don't think that's a typical answer an adult would give in response to an inquiry about potential careers.

I played the best poker face I could and continued with the intake. I noticed his answers were consistently off, and I didn't know what to think. I started thumbing through his intake papers as nonchalantly as possible, but truly desperate to see if there was someone listed as power of attorney for this man, or how I must have missed something in the paperwork. "There is more here than trauma," I thought. Was I going to be able to be of any help to him? This was a typical one-week intensive, and he and his family had incurred the cost of treatment, airline tickets, rental car, hotel and meals all at my word he was appropriate for treatment and would most likely benefit from the experience. Now, less than 20 minutes into Monday morning, I seriously doubted my abilities to help David get more grounded in reality in a week.

When we reached the break for lunch, I asked him if he minded me speaking with the family members who had accompanied him on the trip. He readily agreed and signed the form giving me permission to do so. I told him to take the afternoon off, and I would meet with his relatives. He did so.

After lunch, I met with his family and asked if someone had power of attorney for David. I couldn't imagine he handled his own affairs. They answered that no one did, but were at a loss themselves over his thought processes and reported that before age 15 he had been intelligent, popular and outgoing. There had been a sudden change to isolation and a spiral-downward. He had gone to his parents and reported sexually perpetrating on his numerous siblings. His parents had been shocked and themselves had called in children services to investigate, but upon being interviewed by child protective services, the children had all categorically denied any abuse.   All these years he had remained emotionally stuck. My concern grew exponentially. My performance anxiety was high, and I doubted that much more my ability to help. His history didn't indicate anything significant around age 15. There was nothing to lead me to expect the type of behavior I was seeing from him. These folks were so sincere and earnest for help--help I was almost certain I couldn't give.

When we met the next morning, I asked him if there was anything additional he wanted to put on his trauma list. He assured me there was nothing more. We went to work to address the traumas we had discussed the day before. As we began the processing work, he began to tell me why the trauma we were addressing was actually not difficult and was a very funny situation. I was lost. How did he see this as a trauma yesterday? How did he see this as an event in which he was beyond his normal ability to cope, and now he reported it as amusing? This happened through the next two traumas on the list, as well. It was much like trying to nail Jell-O to the wall. Just when I thought we had some solid bit of work to do that may provide him some reprieve, it would slip through my grasp.

I stopped the work and asked him if he really wanted to be there. I was calm and explained I wouldn't be angry or disappointed, if he decided he didn't want to do this therapy. He assured me he was completely invested. I explained what I'd seen with trauma was that the things included in the processing work were moved off the stage of our minds, but the things we knowingly and intentionally didn't include were left on the center stage in the spotlight. He expressed understanding and assured me again that there was nothing more.

We went to work on yet another story, only to have the same humorous shift at about the halfway point. I sat back and asked him once more about his willingness to participate in treatment. He leaned forward and became intense and stared at the ground. He blurted out that when he was 15, he had viewed some pornographic material and afterwards had an encounter with a friend acting out what he had viewed. Immediately, he raced to the restroom, and I could hear him become sick.

When he returned to the room, I matter-of-factly said what he had shared sounded like a very difficult experience. He seemed a bit taken aback and replied, "Yeah. It really was." I suggested we process it as a trauma. He was agreeable, and we got down to work. Given that as humans we are body, mind and spirit, it stands to reason we are capable of being traumatized in any of those areas. This had been a spiritual trauma for a young teen in a very religious home. The shame and disconnection he had experienced was something for which we are not designed. If I put anything other than 87-octane gasoline in my Jeep, it will damage the engine. We are not made for experiences like the ones he'd had. It didn't matter that there wasn't another person who had perpetrated on him. Trauma treatment isn't about assigning blame, but about addressing the ways a person was hurt through experiences. A leg can be broken all the same, regardless if by accident or intent and so it is with psychological hurt.

Through the NRI model, he was led to reformat his memory as past and to reconnect to himself through the eyes of compassion. The work of connection or reconnection to oneself requires the gift of being known and accepted by another. As therapists, we have the honor of giving that gift to and modeling that gift for clients, so they can grow in self-knowledge and self-acceptance.

The processing of this experience with him was amazing. As he exposed this experience and worked through the horrible misconception of himself as a sexual monster the change in him was astounding. It was like watching shades go up behind his eyes, and there was now light. By that afternoon, as we discussed all sorts of topics, there was a profound clarity and a ready intelligence that had been imperceptible the day before. Whereas the morning prior I was wondering if someone had power of attorney for David, I now could easily see him going on to college and dating. As the week continued, that clarity remained. David's journey wasn't finished. I advised him and his family of different exercises and tasks to improve executive functioning. Trauma causes somewhat of a traffic jam in the limbic system and can prevent a person from developing their ability to problem-solve, prioritize and organize along with the ability to see the link between an action and the outcome. He had missed eight years of brain development and that was evident in things like him choosing to stay up much of the night watching a movie and then being very tired the next day in session. In a way, he was behaving like a 15-year-old boy, but now he was unshackled, and the brain is quite adaptable. He was free to grow.

This experience was a tremendous lesson to me about the power of shame and how crucial our connection to ourselves is. When our self-perception is twisted, we disconnect from the part we disdain. This response fragments our relationship to ourselves and to everyone else, as well, and hampers our ability to engage in life effectively and joyfully.

Charity Starts at Home

Shelly was a three-year-old foster girl who was in a home with her little biological brother. They were to be adopted, however when the foster couple had their own infant baby, Shelly began trying to kill the newborn. I think we all concluded her behavior came out of jealousy because little Shelly's biological mother had been highly negligent, binged on drugs and was often gone for extended periods of time. It was that which led to her being removed from her birth mother's custody. We could only imagine how painful it must be now that she was seeing another little baby get what she didn't get. We could only imagine how painful it must be for her to see another little baby get the nurturing she was denied. None of us really blamed her for being jealous. How could we?

A social worker advocated with the county for me to be allowed to work with the child. Though the county didn't believe it was possible to do therapy with a child that young, they agreed to give it a shot, as it would cost them more to move Shelly and her little brother. During the week of treatment, a total of five hours was spent and about three of those were with the foster mother without Shelly. I needed to help Shelly's caregiver understand trauma and its effects on the brain and how treatment worked, as well as to gather the facts of Shelly's painful past that were known so I could provide thorough help.

While working with Shelly, I used this method of treatment through a directed use of play therapy. She could understand what I was saying to her and that was all I needed. I didn't need her to be able to express herself in words. I used a baby doll to represent the little emotional part of her heart that had endured so much pain. The doll provided a concrete way for us to communicate about something abstract. Towards the end of one session, I picked up the doll and held it to myself and rubbed its back and said that Baby Shelly was now safe. I offered her the doll because it would be important for her to have self-compassion and self-soothe. When I offered her the baby doll, something quite surprising happened. She hauled off and knocked the doll across the room. As she did she yelled, "NO!" I wondered how I was going to get her to embrace what was representing that vulnerable part of her heart. I quickly thought of how viscerally we, especially women, experience the cries of an infant, and I began making a crying sound. "WAAA WAAA." When I did, Shelly's eyes grew as big as saucers. As we were there on the floor in my office, she came right up in my face and covered my mouth with both of her little hands. She was very intense and adamantly said, "NO! NO!!!" over and over again, but I continued to squeak out muffled cries.

Realizing I wasn't going to stop and she couldn't stop me by covering my mouth, she looked for another way to take care of the cries. She went to the doll and picked it up off the floor. I stopped the cries. She threw the doll down. I started the cries again. She picked the doll up and sat on the floor with it. The cries stopped. Down went the baby doll. Back came the cries. We volleyed back and forth for a few minutes until Shelly was finally sitting calmly attentive to the baby doll, holding it and soothing it, holding and soothing her own wounded heart. It was at this point that her attempts on her infant sister's life ended. The adoption was finalized. I learned recently that, these many years later, she's doing wonderfully well and is in a gifted program at her school.

What I learned from that experience was though very young children are concrete in their actions; emotionally they could be very complex. It turned out it wasn't jealousy of her foster sister that led to Shelly's violence towards her. It was actually caused by identifying with her baby sister. It was intolerable to her to perceive

115

the vulnerability that was incarnate in the infant in her foster family and so, Shelly being very concrete and limited in her resources, wanted to make it go away and that's what she had attempted to do.

This lesson was confirmed for me some time later. I was brought adopted identical twins. They had been adopted as babies, and here they were now 12-year-old boys. For the last six years Andrew had been trying to kill Zack. They had spent the first year of their lives in an orphanage and the earliest months in a hospital. When they came to me, Andrew's attempts on his brother were so regular that the parents were not able to let the boys out of their sight. I reasoned it only made sense to begin working with Andrew to try to put an end to the hostile environment.

They were identical twins and I had not met with both of them face to face. I was working at an agency at the time, and these boys had very thick charts. Being the new kid on the block, they got referred on to me, since they had made the rounds of most of the other therapists already. I knew I was the only one there practicing this method of treatment, and the boys had certainly been traumatized. I met with the mother and explained trauma and treatment. She was agreeable to me providing intensive sessions. Andrew had suffered so much as a baby. He had lain in a crib for long periods of time. He had been completely helpless, and his many cries went unheard because of how short-handed the facility was. He had been so alone and vulnerable day in and day out throughout his first year of life. Treatment went along as expected, but by Wednesday morning I still had not cracked the code of his hostility toward Zack. He didn't say anything negative about him. He didn't report any sibling rivalry or even dislike of him. One of the many advantages of intensive treatment is it allows focus on only one or two cases during the week. As I got ready for work on Wednesday, I turned this case inside out in my mind. Then, it hit me.

The day before, the mother of the boys had come to pick up Andrew from his session. She had just received the boy's school pictures that day and asked me if I'd like to see a picture of Zack. Honestly, I wondered why I would need to see a picture of him, if the boys were identical twins. Of course, I would never say that, and so I looked at the photograph. Rather than being impressed by how much the boys looked alike, I was actually struck by how differently they appeared. Certainly, their facial structure was the same. They had the same color hair and eyes, but as it turned out Zack had had kidney problems as a baby and had been born deaf. The ramifications of the early delays were visible in his appearance.

I realized this case was much like the one with Shelly and her baby sister. He, too, had experienced such profound helplessness and vulnerability at the beginning of his life and now had a vulnerable version of himself before his eyes, literally, every day in the body of his weaker identical twin brother. It would be like watching your own vulnerability manifest before you on a day-to-day basis. Who wouldn't want that to end? It would take a very emotionally healthy adult to be able to tolerate that. It would be virtually impossible for a highly traumatized 12-year-old. It must have been emotionally searing for him.

Our integration work that day focused greatly on Andrew's ability to embrace the part of himself that had been so vulnerable.

Once he was able to have compassion for himself, the attempts on his brother's life stopped. It was amazingly simple and amazingly complex at the same time, but it did not take years. The change happened within one week. It was simply a matter of getting to the core of what Andrew was experiencing. Processing his traumas effectively and putting the focus on him having compassion for himself were the keys. He had been in at least six years of therapy that had focused on trying to get him to have compassion for Zack, but that was putting the cart before the horse. He couldn't have compassion for Zack until he had compassion for himself. Health had to start for Andrew the way it does for all of us. It had to start with Andrew being connected to Andrew, and then it was able to flow outwards.

Behavior doesn't change until perception changes. Many traumatized people see the vulnerable part of themselves as bad, weak or stupid. Before processing the trauma, the emotions of the trauma still feel present. Thus, it can easily feel like all we can do is create distance from ourselves or disconnect internally. That's not a consciously thought-out and decided upon approach, but it's what so many people come to nonetheless, leaving us disconnected from ourselves, others and dissatisfied with life. We tend to connect to others to the extent and in the way we connect to ourselves. If we are able to have patience, kindness and understanding towards ourselves, we are able to have those towards others.

10

What's Different About This Method?

Sure, there are a lot of stories of significant transformation that have been laid out here, but what's different about this method, you might be wondering. I'll zoom the camera out and give you a broader perspective. I'll start with giving you an understanding of what typically takes place in traditional therapy. This is what I experienced for 16 years as a client and that in which I was trained through my graduate studies. Individual sessions, of course, are comprised of a licensed mental health clinician and a client. The client presents their symptoms to the therapist and the therapist tries to alleviate those complaints. There is most often a great deal of dialogue used as the primary tool to effect change in and for the client. Since the therapist is the trained professional and the one facilitating the conversation, this makes him or her the leader. Unfortunately, that can often be experienced as the therapist being the source of wisdom and the client being the broken car in the garage to be repaired.

The therapist proceeds to facilitate a discussion with the client and, since the two verbal areas are in the left hemisphere of the brain, the words the client shares are often the left side's take on things. In this way, it's easy for the counseling session to be the therapist's and the client's left hemispheres having a conversation, meaning that analyzing and attempted problem solving can dominate. The difficulty with this, when it comes to trauma treatment, is the right hemisphere is the side through which traumas have been encoded and so the person continues to experience the trauma as a current event. Therefore, even if a client knows where their less optimal behaviors are rooted, that they are now safe, and want to make a change, that is not enough. Remember the amygdala's job is to learn to be afraid. What it has learned to fear and continues to experience as a present threat isn't alleviated simply because the client realizes its origins or a better course of action. *Experiencing* safety is key.

If you or your child have been ever been in counseling, I'm sure you can attest to the fact that you tried everything you could think of along the way. Many people try every sort of behavior chart, token economy or out-and-out bribe for good behavior. Other people try reason, being authoritarian or even abusive, at times, and all to little or no avail. For adults, even highly motivated adults, the results they can eek out of themselves are often no greater.

This is by no means to disrespect or diminish the work of traditional counseling after trauma work is done, but in my 30+

years of combined experience as a client and a clinician, traditional counseling is the wrong tool for the job of trauma processing. There is, however, tremendous benefit traditional counseling could afford the client after trauma treatment. The wonderful and rewarding work of helping a person in healthy human development is finally accessible once the traumas are processed. Picture a traffic jam having been cleared up. The client is now able to accelerate and navigate their journey. On a road trip, that acceleration and navigation might happen automatically, but in the case of trauma, assistance in catching up developmentally and learning how to navigate new options is great work for therapy.

Let's compare this with the NRI method. In the sessions that were provided to the clients whose stories are recounted in this book, the treatment took place because there were symptoms of one sort or another, yes, but not to face-off with or attack those symptoms to eradicate them. Rather, the symptoms were understood as being indicative that the trauma wasn't yet processed effectively. Rather than the therapist playing the role of the one with wisdom and the client being the one with the problem, the client is honored as manifesting wisdom through their behavior. The problem is that wisdom is stuck in the past. For example, Cassie had a self-destructive behavior of cutting, but wasn't seen as self-destructive. I trusted that as we processed her traumas, the traumatic event, which was driving that behavior, would be processed and the symptom would be relieved. In this way, this method of treatment starts from a wellness perspective rather than an illness perspective. We trust each individual is the expert on himself. We see symptoms as expressions of traumatic events encoded as current and manifestations of attempted solutions.

The course of the NRI intensive is one to two weeks of systematically reorganizing traumatic events in the brain's storage. In the beginning, we educate the client (and caregiver, if the client is a child) on how the brain encodes traumas and then work through all the reported traumatic experiences. Integration work goes hand-in-hand through the course of the week so that with the intense emotions of the traumas finally relieved, the client is able to be and become who they really are.

The mental health professional and the client address the traumatic events by executing the systematic method of treatment that reformats those memory files. The therapist is a guide leading the client through treacherous and frightening territory with the skill needed to keep them safe and get them to their destination of experiencing the past as the past. The therapist knows the ongoing experience of those terrible past events as current is the root of the problems and the emotional traffic jam in which the client has been stuck to this point. The client is not fundamentally flawed, broken or bad.

Picture the right hemisphere storage to be like a big bucket of Legos. There are all different colors, sizes and types of pieces. Many of the pieces are dismantled and some are stuck together. Since this big jumbled up mess is consuming so much of the client's energy, we know their left-brain is under-functioning. As therapists with master's level degrees in mental health, we understand the healthy development that ought to have transpired and can recognize clues with precision. Because of our training in trauma, we are able to skillfully serve as the surrogate left-brain for the traumatized client whose left hemisphere is unable to function optimally. In this way, we are able to help the client effectively transform the disarray of the pile of trauma pieces into an organized story, finally reformatted the way it needs to be so it's experienced as past, not just identified as past.

The therapist also serves as a facilitator of group therapy for the competing and conflicting thoughts and feelings within the individual. We serve as a supporter to the healthy, compassionate part of the client so she can begin to relate to herself in a healthy way. Through the integration work, we teach clients to pay attention to what the concerned or controlling parts need to have heard, but leading the client into living from a place of love rather than fear.

NRI treatment, in short, is a systematic process of recoding memories. First, a thorough trauma history is gathered. Each trauma is put through the process of creating a re-telling of the story according to the components of the instinctual response we have to traumatic events. This is done through drawing for adults and children old enough to draw. For children too young to draw, this is accomplished through the use of directed play therapy. Each important aspect of the trauma is included in the trauma story and the thoughts, emotions and body sensations that go along with each of the scenes are expressed, as well. Video is used to capture the re-telling of the story (not the client), so it can be viewed back by the client, allowing for a removed perspective that is contained and in a historical context. From the removed perspective the client can have compassion for their hurt self. We glean from each story the positive qualities that can be seen about the client from each one of the traumas. The client gains not only a new experience of the event, but of himself, as well. The integration work on each one of the traumas helps the client to shift from the part of them that has been stuck in the continual experience of the trauma to the wise self who now is able to navigate their way forward, unburdened. Throughout the process, the therapist often plays the role of the client's advocate and surrogate left brain, since many times the client is rejecting of their hurt self and unable to do optimal problem solving and reasoning. The foundation of the NRI model is that of connection to self and others. Connection is the purpose of and foundation for our approach and what drives growth after treatment. Often, people tend to wonder if there might be something traumatic they endured that they have buried beyond their consciousness. Actually, what we find is people minimize the effects of what they know they experienced. Once those things are sufficiently addressed, they often experience relief.

It would be an easy, but dangerous mistake to attempt to provide this treatment without the foundation of a master's degree in a mental health field and a certification in NRI. Though the method may look simple to someone on the outside, it is impossible to begin to articulate the thousands of micro-decisions a certified and licensed therapist is making through the course of treatment. The required training allows us to elegantly navigate the obstacles in such a way that makes the process look simple.

A comparison of what is traditionally known as counseling and NRI is shown in Figure 10.

Figure 10 – NRI/Traditional Therapy

NRI	Traditional Therapy
Works on the amygdala	Works on the cortex
Directed use of non-verbal expressive therapy	Uses language and reasoning
Focuses directly and intentionally on the client's traumatic experiences	Focuses on emotions and behavior
Systematic and comprehensive reformatting of the traumas, so they are experienced as past	Follows the problems that have arisen since the last session
Usually one week	Often lasts for years
Brief/time limited	Indefinite
Addresses trauma at its biological roots	Generally deals with the presenting problem
Can be provided to preverbal clients	Not typically provided to preverbal children
Helps the client directly unpack traumatic experiences without re-experiencing it	Often causes intense emotion in trying to directly address traumas
Works on the neurological level	Works on the conscious awareness level
Increases the client's ability to experience traumas as past events	Not generally effective to resolve trauma

125

11

Where Do I Go From Here?

If you are the caregiver of a child who has been through traumatic events, there are some things in your power that can be beneficial for the child both before and after they are able to receive NRI treatment. Please understand the efficacy of these tips will be limited as long as there is unprocessed trauma.

Caregiver Tips

- ❖ Address only the "wise"/cooperative part of the child from your true self. That is, relate True Self to True Self, as was shown in the triangles.

- ❖ Do not make the child responsible for your emotions. Relate to the child out of calm compassion and encourage them to relate to themselves the same way.

- ❖ Be calm and assertive. If you cannot be and stay calm and assertive, look at and address why you cannot. If you have your own unprocessed traumas, then get help for yourself, too. You deserve it.

❖ Affirm and accentuate the positive minute-by-minute, hour-by-hour, and day-by-day.

❖ The child fundamentally wants to feel safe. When behavior is oppositional, angry, and defiant, calmly and compassionately reassure the child he is emotionally and physically safe.

❖ Give free choices between true options whenever possible and affirm the choice that is made.

❖ Create "no fail" situations that do not have any objective other than BEING one-on-one together with the child. This is time to develop relationship – not to reprimand or give directives.

❖ Have and keep clear house rules with clear privileges and consequences. This helps to prevent the caregiver and child from feeling the day is unpredictable and instead provides a sense of security.

❖ Focus on affirming and enjoying the child rather than being afraid of or for him/her or controlling their behavior. The better the child feels about himself the more he will control his own behavior.

❖ Be the leader. Do not wait for your child to set the tone for the day. Treat oppositional behavior directly and immediately, yet calmly and compassionately with the agreed upon consequences and don't hold a grudge. If you're holding a grudge, take a look at what that's about in you and address it or get the help you need to forgive the child, remembering their behaviors are not about you.

❖ Being frustrated is normal. Be frustrated with the behavior and not with the child. If he becomes frustrated with himself as well, his behavior will only worsen and compound the problem.

Treatment

Some of the many different types of traumas treated with NRI are listed below.

Typical Traumas Treated

In Utero Trauma
Birth Trauma
Physical Abuse
Emotional Abuse
Verbal Abuse
Sexual Abuse
Rape
Sex-Trafficking
Violent Crimes
Combat
Domestic Violence
Neglect
Removal from Biological Caregiver(s)
Foster Home Placements/Moves
Witnessing Abuse or Violent Crime
Automobile/Sports Accidents
Natural Disasters
School Shootings
Terrorism

Some of the symptoms and diagnoses that diminish when the traumas are treated with NRI are listed below.

Typical Symptoms

Anxiety
Depression

Low Self-Esteem
Difficulty Connecting to Others
Difficulties Relating in the Classroom
Difficulties Making Friends
Argumentative/Defiant/Oppositional Behaviors
Avoidant/Escape Behaviors
Self Harm
Physical Symptoms that don't respond to medical interventions
Regression (seemingly stuck at an age/stage younger than one is or in particular fears/worries)

Typical Diagnoses

Generalized Anxiety Disorder
Depressive Disorders
Post-traumatic Stress Disorder
Dissociative Disorders
Attachment Disorders
Phobias
Obsessive-Compulsive Disorder
Oppositional Defiant Disorder
Conduct Disorder
Attention Deficit Disorder/Attention Deficit Hyperactivity Disorder

Over the last decade, many people have asked me the best way to approach treatment. Here are some strategies I've found that will help you make the most of treatment for a child or for yourself.

What about missing school for treatment? At times caregivers have expressed concern about their child missing school for intensive NRI treatment. What we have found is the process of treatment benefits the child's ability to be successful in the classroom. Most often, emotional, cognitive, behavioral, and relational improvements we see through the course of treatment make the time missed in the classroom a well-rewarded trade.

Provide a thorough history. One of the most helpful things you can do whether for your own treatment or that of your child is to provide a thorough history from pregnancy to present day with as much as is known. That's not to say you have to have all the details for treatment to be beneficial, but the more information we have the more clues we have to providing thorough help.

Prepare your child for treatment. I have always recommended that caregivers tell their children that the purpose of treatment is to make stories about the times they had to be brave. Bravery isn't an emotion. It's a sign of strength when tested by fearful circumstances. Preparing the child in this way bespeaks your own validation of their difficult stories and best primes them for understanding we see them as brave survivors, not a collection of symptoms.

Courageously approach your own treatment. If you are coming for treatment yourself, I highly encourage you to be open about your trauma history and your current sticking points. Since leaving traumas unprocessed stands to mitigate the benefits of treatment, you certainly want to be open about your trauma history so it can be thoroughly addressed. Also, there have been numerous times people have come for treatment and not been forthcoming about less than optimal behaviors that were causing them difficulty. Sadly, that left them with less help than they deserved. Any good mental health therapist will not judge you. In this treatment, be assured we see unhealthy behaviors, compulsions and addictions as attempts to solve the problems resulting from how traumas are stored.

Choose your battles through the week of treatment. Compassion and understanding from you toward your child's behaviors through their intensive week will greatly help the focus of therapy to remain focused on trauma processing. If you are getting treatment for yourself, try to limit your outside distractions.

Protect the therapeutic alliance between the therapist and your child. If there is something that transpires since the child's session on the previous day, please email or call the therapist to fill them in about it in private. If you bring the child in for treatment and scold the child in front of the therapist or ask the therapist to scold the child, you will jeopardize the therapeutic relationship. We tend to hide when we feel shame and so the child will tend to shutdown and not be as forthcoming as we need them to be.

Follow through on treatment recommendations. Make sure you make the most of treatment by following the recommendations your therapist will give you for post-treatment growth. After treatment, if you recall a trauma you or your child forgot to process, get back in the office to make sure it is addressed.

Seek health in all areas of life. I'm always encouraged when people are seeking health in all areas of their lives, physical, emotional and spiritual. It is unfair to a child to fill them full of sugar, give them little in the way of physical outlets for their energy, but expect them to be calm and composed. Our bodies simply don't work that way. One facet of our lives can drag another down, when it remains unhealthy. On the flipside, they all benefit each other when working optimally.

Give feedback and spread the word. One of the greatest gifts to me over the years has been the feedback of the clients and caregivers with whom I've had the great honor and pleasure to work. It is their stories that filled this book and afforded me access to knowledge I would not otherwise have had. Their feedback helped me provide the most thorough treatment possible and detect when the processing of a trauma had been overlooked. Their willingness to tell others about the help they received has allowed this method to spread.

Encourage your therapist to get certified in NRI. Over the years I have treated clients who have come from all across the nation and outside of the country. It has been profoundly edifying to witness people going to whatever lengths needed to get the help they need. My desire is for this method to be available for hurting people everywhere.

Further Training

If you are a caregiver, teacher, coach, pastor or in any other way care for traumatized children or are a licensed mental health clinician desiring training in this work, please go to our webpage at www.thrivetraininginstitute.com for information and to follow our blog.

If you are licensed mental health practitioner with a master's degree or higher, I strongly recommend certification in this model of treatment. Although I wouldn't have had the strength or courage to choose to go through the traumas I did, I consider having been introduced to the roots of this method of treatment as a crucially transformative factor in my life both personally and professionally.

There are many aspects to a healthy life and relating that are open to people once traumas are processed. Stay in touch for more information on these topics and recommendations for post-treatment growth.

Treatment

If you are interested in treatment through this method, please visit us at www.finallythrive.org for more information.

Be courageous! Freedom awaits you! YOU were born to THRIVE!

About the Author

A native of Brunswick, Georgia, Margaret Vasquez received her education at Franciscan University, Steubenville, OH. She became a licensed professional clinical counselor, certified trauma therapist and certified intensive trauma therapy instructor. The developer of NRI (Neuro-Reformatting and Integration), Margaret's approach utilizes the Instinctual Trauma Response model of trauma treatment from the perspective of connection. She has appeared on numerous television and radio shows and presents regularly to foster and adoptive parents, mental health clinicians and professionals working with trauma populations. She is the founder and director of Thrive Trauma Recovery and Thrive Training Institute. Margaret's passion is for people to maximize their potential.

Made in the USA
Middletown, DE
20 August 2021

46487427R00092